TRADING OPTIONS FOR BEGINNERS 2020

****

A Guide To Make Money With Trading Options: A Crash Course For Success. Create Passive Income Using Simple Strategies, Discipline, And Psychology To Start Investing

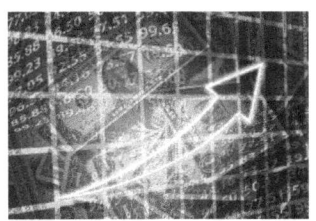

By: Oliver J. Rich

© **Copyright 2019 - All Rights Reserved**

This document is geared towards providing exact and reliable information in regards to the topic and issue covered. The publication is sold with the idea that the publisher is not required to render accounting, officially permitted, or otherwise, qualified services. If advice is necessary, legal or professional, a practiced individual in the profession should be ordered.

- From a Declaration of Principles which was accepted and approved equally by a Committee of the American Bar Association and a Committee of Publishers and Associations.

It is, in no way, legal to reproduce, duplicate, or transmit any part of this document in either electronic means or in printed format. Recording of this publication is strictly prohibited and any storage of this document is not allowed unless with written permission from the publisher. All rights reserved.

The information provided herein is stated to be truthful and consistent. Any liability, in terms of inattention or otherwise, by any usage or abuse of any policies, processes, or directions contained within is the solitary and utter responsibility of the recipient reader.

Under no circumstances will any legal responsibility or blame be held against the publisher for any reparation, damages, or monetary loss due to the information herein, either directly or indirectly.

Respective authors own all copyrights not held by the publisher.

The information herein is offered for informational purposes solely and is universal as so. The presentation of the information is without a contract or any type of guarantee assurance.

The trademarks that are used are without any consent and the publication of the trademark is without permission or backing by the trademark owner. All trademarks and brands within this book are for clarifying purposes only and are owned by the owners themselves, not affiliated with this document.

WHY YOU NEED THIS BOOK

Puts, calls, strike prices, prices, derivatives, bear place spreads, Nd bull phone spreads -- the jargon describes the complex areas of options buying and selling. However, do not allow some of it frighten you away.

Options can offer flexibility for traders at every degree and support them in managing danger. Listed below are the fundamentals of what options are, why investors utilize them, and how to begin.

No matter what you are doing in life there's always the first moment. Walking as a child, worries, or starting a new job all belong to this category. That is correct of beginner's options buying and selling in the currency markets as well. Even though you have experience in stock trading you can't possibly be expected to know the distinction between a call-up and a place; don't get bothered, because this is not going to result in a pop quiz. In the following pages, you can look at options investing for beginners and examine a number of the basics to truly get you started. When you have never been subjected to options trading, here you are for your first time!

In Options Trading for Beginners, we are concerned with the basics - the fundamentals of a strong foundation in learning the stock options trade. E uipped with the proper knowledge, you can gain massive profits from stock options. It can be difficult for beginners in option trading to learn the exact difference between trading in the stock market and trading in the stock options market.

Because of the time limits set on each trade, many beginners in option trading have a common misconception that stock options are associated with significant risks. The time limit is often seen as a waste of assets. Options trading has proven to be profitable with those traders who go into it with a plan and the knowledge of effective leveraging techniques. Options tend to be chosen for the level of leverage versus the limited amount of risk.

Contents

WHY YOU NEED THIS BOOK......4
INTRODUCTION 8
    PUT OPTION 35
    JUST HOW DO PUT OPTIONS FUNCTION? 37
CHAPTER 1 42
    THE BASICS OF OPTIONS TRADING PROFITABILITY......42
CHAPTER 2 74
    IN THE MONEY (ITM) 74
CHAPTER 3 81
    OUT OF THE MONEY (OTM)......81
CHAPTER 4......107
    THE BASICS OF OPTION TRADING PRICES......107
CHAPTER 5......112
    CHOOSING THE RIGHT OPTION 112
CHAPTER 6......114
    OPTION TRADING TIPS AND STRATEGIES......114
CHAPTER 7......152
    USING OPTIONS FOR SPECULATION 152
CHAPTER 8......155
    HOW TO START TRADING OPTIONS 155
    PUT YOUR PREDICTORS' CAP ON 181
CONCLUSION......194

INTRODUCTION

What Are Options?

Options are conditional derivative agreements that allow purchasers of the accords (alternative holders) to get or sell off a security at a chosen price. Option buyers priced an amount referred to as a "high quality" by sellers for this type of right. Should industry prices become unfavorable for option holders, they will let the option expire worthless, therefore ensuring the deficits are not higher than the premium. On the other hand, option writers assume higher risk compared to the option buyers, which explains why they require this premium.

Options can be bought like most various other asset groups with brokerage investment decision accounts.

Options are reliable since they can enhance a person's portfolio. They do that through added cash flow, protection, and also leverage. Depending on the situation, there is usually a option scenario befitting an investor's target. A simplified example of this would be employing options as a useful hedge against declining currency markets to control downside losses. Alternatives could also be used to generate repeating income. Additionally, they are generally helpful for speculative purposes, such as wagering on the direction of a stock.

Options are among the most popular derivatives for stock traders, because their price tag can move quickly, making (or getting rid of) big money fast. Options techniques can range between reasonably simple to highly complex, with several payoffs and in some cases odd titles.

A option is a contract to get or sell off a stock, typically 100 shares on the stock per agreement, for a pre-negotiated value and by way of a specific date.

Just as you can purchase a stock as you think the purchase price will rise or sell a stock once you think its price tag will drop, an option lets you bet on which direction you think the price tag on a stock will go. But, instead of shopping for or shorting the stock outright, once you buy a option, you're investing in a contract which allows -- but doesn't obligate -- one to do a number of things, like:

Buy or sell off shares of shares at an agreed-upon selling price (the "hit selling price") for a restricted time frame;

Sell the agreement to another buyer; or

Let the alternative agreement expire and leave without further monetary obligation.

Trading options are of help for long-term buy-and-hold traders, too.

Options trading for beginners can seem to be a daunting task. Words like delta, volatility, and premium scare many investors. Are you looking to start in the options trading market, and following a few easy steps will make the task a bit more manageable?

With stocks and bonds, there is nothing like free lunch. Options are the same. Options trading includes certain risks that the investor must know about before making an exchange. This is the reason, when trading options with a dealer, you more often than not observe a disclaimer like the following:

"Significant: Options include risks and are not reasonable for everybody. Options trading can be theoretical in nature and convey generous risk of misfortune".

Options as Derivatives

Options have a place within the larger category of assets known as derivatives. A derivative's cost is reliant on or gotten from the cost of something different. For instance, wine is a derivative of grapes, ketchup is a derivative of tomato, and a stock option is a derivative of a stock. Options are derivatives of money-related protections—their worth relies upon the cost of some other asset. Instances of derivatives incorporate calls, puts, futures, advances, swaps, and home loan supported protections, among others.

Options are a particular sort of derivatives contracts. The fundamental protections can be stocks, records, ETFs, or wares. With a derivatives contract, you don't legitimately own the primary asset. Instead, you own a related asset whose worth is influenced by changes in the price of the primary asset.

With an options contract, you reserve the option to purchase or sell an asset at a preordained cost later on. When that future point arrives, you will have the decision to practice the option or let it terminate.

Here's a model. Suppose the asset is selling for $110. An agreement giving you the privilege to purchase that asset at $100 will have inherent worth. As the expiration date draws near, the worth of the options contract will change.

Types of Options

Call Option - Option to buy the fundamental asset.

Put Option - Option to sell the fundamental asset.

Options Contract - The understanding between the author and the purchaser.

Vanilla Option - An ideal option with no extraordinary highlights, terms, or conditions.

American Option - Option that can be practiced at any time before the expiration date.

European Option - Option that can be practiced only on the expiration date.

Exotic Option - Any option with a mind boggling structure or result estimation.

American and European Options

American options can be practiced at any time between the date of procurement and the expiration date. European options are not quite the same as American options, in that they may only be practiced on their expiration date. The differentiation between American and European options has nothing to do with topography, just with early work out. Numerous options on stocks are of the European kind. Because the privilege to practice early has some worth, an American option typically conveys a higher premium than a generally indistinguishable European option. This is because the early exercise feature is attractive and demands a premium.

American option

An American option is a put option or call option that can be practiced at any time before its expiration date.

How it functions/Example:

For instance, an investor holding an American option that expires on the last Friday in March has the privilege to practice that option whenever at the very latest that date.

Because the option value moves in a state of harmony with the underlying asset, the worth of the option may rise and fall on various occasions over the life of the agreement. The greater part of the options that exchange on real exchanges are American options.

With an American option, the holder can trust that the most effective cost will practice the option. He can exercise the option on any of the trading days up to the expiration date. Because of more noteworthy adaptability, American options are more profitable than European-style options, which must be exercised on the date of expiration.

European option

A European option is a sort of put or call option that can be practiced uniquely on its expiration date.

How it functions/Example:

Assume an investor, John, purchases a European call option on March first that terminates on the third Friday in March. During the second seven day stretch of March, the estimation of the primary asset transcends the strike cost. The holder of an European option can't make the most of this fleeting chance to secure a benefit, because the only date he can trade this option is on its expiration date.

Conversely, American options may be practiced whenever from the date of procurement until expiration. The holder of an American option may choose that the estimation of his option has arrived at its best point, regardless of whether development, or the date of expiration, has not come. Such an option could then be sold before development.

The proprietor of an European option, however, must wait until development. In the model above, John may find that the European option is worth less at development than when he bought it. In the event that he held an American option, he might have the option to make a benefit prior to the date of expiration in the life of the option.

European options more often than not exchanged at a markdown to their American counterparts because there is only a solitary chance to practice the option. However, if the holder of the European option would not like to hold the option until the expiration date, he should close his situation by selling the option. These options exchange predominantly over-the-counter and are, once in a while, observed on the real exchanges

Vanilla Option

A vanilla option refers to an ordinary option with no uncommon highlights, terms, or conditions.

How it functions/Example:

Options are available in an assortment of "flavors." A plain vanilla option offers the privilege to buy or sell a basic security by a specific date at a set strike cost. In contrast with other option structures, vanilla options are not extravagant or muddled. Such options might be outstanding in the business sectors, and simple to exchange.

Progressively, in any case, the term "vanilla option" is a general proportion of a multifaceted nature, particularly where investors are considering different options and structures.

Option structures might be mind-boggling. Be that as it may, in options trading, at times, straightforward option structures might be justified. Note that vanilla options don't show lower execution or opportunity.

Exotic Option

There are also exotic options, which are called exotic because there may be a minor departure from the result profiles of the plain vanilla options. They can turn out to be entirely unexpected items all together with "optionality" implanted in them.

An exotic option is any option contract involving credits not regular to most contracts which result in different valuation plans. It is something contrary to a plain vanilla option.

How it functions/Example:

Exotic options contain complex criteria influencing valuation and result. As a rule, these criteria are time-delicate and enable the holder to practice explicit inclinations at different points before the expiration date. Instances of exotic options incorporate Asian options (strike cost depends on the anticipated standard cost of the primary asset over a particular interim) and compound options (underlying asset is another option). Exotic options ought not be mistaken for plain vanilla options, which just contain a specific strike value, expiration date, and fundamental asset.

For instance, two-fold options have a basic result structure that is resolved if the result occasion happens, paying little respect to the degree. Different kinds of exotic options include thump out, thump in, hindrance options, lookback options, Asian options, and Bermudan options. Once more, exotic options are typically for expert derivatives dealers.

The complexities related with exotic options make them hard to exchange on a trade. Thus, most exotic options are exchanged through an over-the-counter (OTC) showcase.

The two principle kinds of options

There are two distinct kinds of options - call options, and put options. When utilized effectively, options trading can make your investing methodology considerably more powerful. How about we plunge into the following area.

Options are a kind of derivative security. An option is a derivative because its cost is intrinsically connected to the cost of something different. In the event that you purchase an options contract, it awards you the right, however not the commitment, to purchase or sell a primary asset at a set cost before a specific date.

Regardless of their complexity, all options strategies are based on the two basic types of options: the call and the put.

Call Options

Call options are money-related contracts that give the option purchaser the right, yet not the commitment, to purchase a stock, security, product, or other asset or instrument at a predetermined cost during a particular time span. The stock, bond, or commodity is called the hidden asset. A call purchaser benefits when the fundamental asset increases in value.

A call option differs from a put, which gives the holder the privilege to sell the hidden asset at a predetermined cost before expiration.

What is a Call Option?

A Call Option gives you the privilege to buy a asset in the future. Whenever worked out, this buy will happen on a preordained date. It will likewise happen at a preordained worth. In the event that you are uncertain about the future estimated value of an asset, a call option can offer some assurance. Stock dealers generally buy call options. Be that as it may, they can be found in numerous different markets. Actually, call options are the most ordinarily exchanged options contracts.

A call option gives the holder the privilege to purchase a stock. Think of a call option as a down-payment for a future purpose. With a call option, the buyer of the contract acquires the right to buy the underlying asset in the future at a predetermined price, called the exercise price or strike price.

A call option is known as the agreement between a buyer and a seller regarding the purchase of a stock at an agreed on price up until a defined expiration date. The buyer has the right, but not the obligation, to exercise the call and buy the stock. The seller must deliver the stock if the option is exercised.

A hypothetical call option contract could give a buyer the right to buy 100 shares of a company for $100 each. In this case, $100 is what is referred to as the strike price. Until the option contract expires, the option buyer has the right to those shares at that agreed price regardless of the stock market price. Any appreciation above that strike price represents profit for the buyer. If the price shoots up to $150 then the buyer has made a total profit of $5,000, less the cost of the option.

The call option buyer has to pay a fee known as the premium to the seller. In the case above, imagine the premium is $4. This means the premium total of $400 ($4 x 100 shares) would leave a profit of $4,600. However, if the stock instead declined in value, the buyer would have no reason to exercise the right to buy the stock for the higher cost. They would more than likely choose to allow the contract to expire and lose the $400. Or, they could sell the option, if it still has value, to avoid taking a full loss.

But this "full loss" is less than it seems. If you bought the underlying asset itself instead, say 100 shares for $100 each, even a $5 decline would result in losing more money. As this example shows, the option limits the risk.

In addition to the premium, commissions and fees can also add to the overall expense of options trading. That can be sizable.

Another example is if a potential property holder sees another advancement going up. That individual may need the privilege to buy a home in the future, yet will just need to practice that privilege once specific improvements around the region are assembled.

The potential home purchaser would profit by obtaining the option of purchasing or not. Envision they can purchase a call option from the designer to purchase the home for $400,000 anytime in the following three years.

The potential home purchaser needs to contribute a initial installment to secure that right.

Concerning an option, this expense is known as the premium. It is the cost of the option contract. In our home model, the initial installment may be $20,000 that the purchaser pays the designer. Suppose two years have passed and now the advancements are assembled, and zoning has been endorsed. The home purchaser trades the option and purchases the home for $400,000 because it's the agreement acquired.

The market estimation of that home may have multiplied to $800,000. But, because the up front installment secured a pre-decided value, the purchaser pays $400,000. In another situation, suppose the zoning endorsement doesn't come until the fourth-year of this option. The home purchaser must pay the market cost because the agreement has terminated. In either case, the designer keeps the first $20,000 gathered.

What Is A Long Call Option?

When you have buy a call option, it means you have the right to purchase shares. It's referred to as being "long a call." Because a long call costs a fraction of the underlying stock price, there is more potential upside on a percentage basis than buying the underlying security itself.

What Does Long Call Mean?

What is the meaning of long call? Long calls offer a critical development potential and investors acknowledge gains when the market value transcends the strike cost; for example, the value that the option is worked out. There is likewise a premium that investors pay to buy a long call which is, really, the expense of the option understanding. At the point when investors expect or guess an ascent in the stock costs, they purchase a call option in light of the fact that the likelihood of the market going up is high.

Conversely, if the market value drops lower than the strike value, the long call holders lose the cash they paid to enter the option understanding in addition to the premium. In this manner, a long call limits risk to the sum paid for the call and has a boundless development potential.

Model

Abis claims 250 portions of a development organization, which presently exchange at $105. Abis believes that the stock cost will increase on the grounds that the organization has finished a gainful arrangement with a focused firm. The market feels that this arrangement will support the gainfulness of the two organizations.

Abis needs to expand his situation in the stock; however, he has no cash. To purchase another 100 shares would cost him $10,500. Conse☐uently, he buys a long call with a strike cost of $130, expecting that the stock cost will transcend the strike cost before development, which is in 35 days. The option is evaluated at $3, so Abis pays $300 and purchases 100 portions of the basic stock.

In the event that the stock value ascends to $165, Abis has the privilege to trade his call option and purchase 100 shares for $130 and sell them in the open market for $165, along these lines understanding an increase of ($165 x 100) − ($130 x 100) = $3,500. In this way, his net benefit is $3,500 − $300 = $3,200.

If the stock value unlikely drops to $125, Abis loses the $300 that he paid for the long call.

What Is A Short Call Option?

When a call option is sold, you receive payment for the call and are obligated to sell shares of the underlying stock at the strike price until the expiration date. This is also known as writing or being short. While you can create income by selling call options via the premium, there is risk if the stock price rises above the strike price. And, given the overall tendency of the stock market to go up, this risk is not insubstantial.

When you brief a call option, you're advertising it before you get it. That converts the whole transfer around, so you make money only when the alternative call price drops ahead of contract expiration.

It's much like shorting inventory except you've got a deadline (the time the contract expires).

Remember: you get a credit back immediately once you short a stock. That credit can be your maximum revenue.

If the underlying stock's price is higher than the strike cost at expiration, it's in the amount of money. That means the one who bought that call up option from you'll expect you to sell shares on the underlying stock to her or him at the strike price.

You will have to buy shares of the stock in order to complete that purchase. Because the stock option is the amount of money, you'll market those stocks for an instantaneous loss.

Remember: in the event, the stock rises dramatically, you'll have a significant loss. A short call is a very dangerous approach because your damage is unlimited.

If the rootstock remains below the strike price at agreement expiration, then your alternative expires worthless. You retain the premium you earned from sale of the option and create a nice profit.

What Is A Covered Call Option?

With short call options, consider the difference between covered and uncovered calls. The latter instrument is also called a naked call.

When your short call is covered, you already own the shares you are obliged to sell. The worst that can happen is that you are forced to sell your stock at a lower price. But, even though they are being compensated with the premium, investors can find it tough psychologically if there is a big move in a stock they own when they know they will take none of the gains.

There are several benefits from this options trading approach for people who own stocks.

"In this case, the investor could be collecting income, while also defining an exit price (to sell the underlying at a predetermined price) and simultaneously partly offsetting a decline, should that occur,". "Covered calls can allow investors to lower the cost basis of a long position since the income received from the sale effectively lowers the acquisition price."

An uncovered short call or naked call means you are betting on stock you do not even own. Here there is a theoretical potential for unlimited losses.

This is because you are obligated to sell shares. You might have to buy them on the open market at a much higher price and sell them for the lower agreed upon price of the option contract. The difference between those prices can end up resulting in a sizable loss to your account.

Why do traders use covered calls?

A covered call is employed by traders who are fundamentally bullish and believe the underlying asset will rise steadily, or not beyond a specific price point. Under these circumstances, the trader is able to make a profit from both the long position and the short call position.

This enables the trader to secure a higher return than would be possible from holding the long position alone. If their bullish view is incorrect, the short call serves as a hedge to offset some of the trader's losses that are incurred as a result of the asset falling in value.

How do covered calls work?

Covered calls work because a trader who currently holds a long position on an asset gives up their right to sell that asset at any time for the market value. Instead, under the obligations of a call option, they must sell the asset to the buyer at the expiry date for the strike price – so long as the buyer exercises their right to buy.

From the call seller's perspective, they can only be worried if the underlying asset price rises to levels higher than the strike, at which point the buyer can be expected to trade the option. However, if the sellers are already long on the underlying instrument, they would already be profiting from the upward move.

Buyers of calls will typically exercise their right to buy if the underlying price exceeds a pre-determined strike price at or before a given expiry date. If the underlying price does not reach this strike level, the buyer will likely not trade their option because the underlying asset will be cheaper on the open market.

Covered call example

Let's suppose a trader owns 100 shares in company ABC, which they think have a strong chance of generating profit in the long term. But in the short term, they expect the share price to fall – or to not increase dramatically – from the current price of £50.

As a result, the trader decides to sell a call option on the same stock with a strike price of £60. They will earn a premium by selling this call option, but they will cap the total upside potential of their share investment at £60 – or a £10 profit per share.

In this example, let's assume that the premium for this call option is 100p per share. Since options are always traded in lots of 100 shares, the trader stands to receive a total premium of £100.

The trader will generate a profit for all gains up to a share price of £60 after which any additional profits will be offset by losses incurred on the short call option. This is because the price of it is now above the stated strike, meaning the option is 'in-the-money'.

As a result, the maximum the trader stands to gain is the £100 premium, plus £10 profit per share. So, their total profit is capped at £1100 (for an underlying share price of £60 or higher) because they own 100 shares.

Now, if the share price rises to levels greater than £60, the trader will not realise these additional gains – or to be more accurate, gains in the long ABC position have been offset by losses on the short call.

However, for lesser upward movements, or drops in share price, the premium obtained by selling the call serves as a useful source of revenue, either to increase profits or to mitigate losses.

Covered call Strategies

Here are some ⬜uick strategies you should use with covered calls: some connect with blue chips shares, others to high-risk organizations, and some for all those stocks that you expect minimal increases.

1. Boosting Dividends

Buying stocks and promoting options contracts decreases your ade⬜uate expense basis. Furthermore, you will nevertheless collect 100% on the dividends from firms who present these payments. Because of this, selling options agreements increase your dividend produces. Below, an example:

You get Nutrisystem (NASDAQ: NTRI) stocks, which give quarterly dividends at $0.175 per share, at the current value of $14.24.

You then offer call options that expire in 9 weeks with an effective price of $10 per share that are respected at $4.50.

You receive a instantaneous come back of $4.50, which reduces your net price per share to $9.74.

As explained in this book, share rates can fall practically 32%, from $14.24 for your net expense of $9.74, without the capital loss staying incurred.

Furthermore, at your brand-new cost groundwork of $9.74 per share, your yearly dividend yield increases from 5% to 7.2%. Therefore, while you have limited your money increase upside, you also have significantly raised your dividend produce. This is a very useful strategy unless you think the actual stock price can make a huge profit, or if you're pretty opposed to threat and desire to profit typically from dividends while developing a 32% hedge against dropping share prices.

2. Adding Income Steady stream to Funds Gains

Another solution to play covered calls is to establish the strike value above the current price. You'll do this in the event that you expect share costs to appreciate reasonably. In so doing, you benefit from both a growth in share costs and the excess revenue from advertising the options. Beneath is an illustration:

You predict that stocks of Ford (NYSE: F), which now sells at $15.28, will rise over the upcoming 3 months.

You own shares at $15.28 each.

You offer a call option agreement for $0.29 per share which will expire in a few months with a strike price of $17 per share.

If share rates rise, you're allowed to keep the capital gains around the $17 hit price tag, or $1.72 per share. Furthermore, you also acquire

29 cents per share from selling the decision options contract. This can boost earnings by 7.6% on the year (predicated on annualizing the few months call options agreement cost of 29 cents). Needless to say, your capital profits may also be capped if share prices create a huge profit beyond the $17 strike price.

3. Hedging Chance with Volatile Stocks

Risk goes far up if you hold in volatile stocks. Obtaining call or put options for speculative buying and selling may also be high priced because options derive a lot of their value from volatility. When this happens, you can purchase the inventory and sell call options which are "deep in the amount of money" to safeguard against a substantial decrease in inventory price tag. "Deep in the amount of money" refers to when the strike price is nicely below the actual price. Conse☐uently, you create some security against a downward slide and a decent upside increase. Consider this case in point to observe how it is completed:

Solar stocks include high possiblities but are correspondingly risky. One such stock, Energy Conversion Products (NASDAQ: ENER), trades at $2.02 per share presently.

You get 100 stocks at $2.02 per share.

You offer a call option contract which has a $1.00 strike value for $1.27 per share and expires in a few months.

Your effective expense basis per share can be $0.75 at present.

Your maximum benefit is definitely $0.25 per share or the variation between your cost and the strike price.

How is this top upside calculated? As your strike price is defined at $1.00, you might have necessarily offered the rights on your own inventory above this volume. To put this yet another way, you will preserve ownership around $1.00. If the price eventually ends up above $1.00, the options will undoubtedly be exercised. Your prospective reward may be the difference between your $0.75 of share cost along with the $1.00 of settlement once the options will be applied at any volume above this. Consequently, even if present prices slip to $1.00 (or perhaps a 50% shed from when you purchased it) plus the rights aren't exercised, you'll still have built a 33% gain converting 75 cents into profit. This is an excellent strategy if you are dedicated to a inventory that you think has a significant probability to suffer a substantial decrease in cost.

The covered call strategy is common among long-term traders who want to amplify their profits on shares they own. In the event that you know very well what a covered call is and how you can properly put into action this options buying and selling strategy, it is possible to increase your inventory portfolio rapidly.

With a covered call, additionally, you get some drawback protection. However, the blissful luxury of experiencing this downside security includes an expense of capping the upside earnings probable on those long shares.

PUT OPTION

A Put Option offers you the right to market an asset in the foreseeable future. Like call options, these agreements have predetermined rates and sell times. Put options and call options tend to be purchased together to make a "hedged" posture. Below, we shall discuss the various forms of options sales. We shall then talk about how these product sales can be incorporated into your buying and selling strategy.

Put options give the holder the right to sell a stock. With a put option, the buyer acquires the right to sell the underlying asset in the future at the predetermined price.

For clarity's sake, it is worth mentioning the difference between a call option and a put option. Basically, the latter is the exact opposite of the former. A put option gives the investor the option to sell a stock at an agreed price before or on a specified date. This can be used to protect your stock gains against a fall in price.

"If you are long stock or an ETF that has risen in value, you may want to protect your gains," the Options Industry Council's Prosperi said. "One way to do so would be by purchasing a put, which is often referenced as similar to insurance."

Purchasing a PUT option on a stock gives the buyer the option, but not the obligation, to sell a stock at a fixed price until a set date.

Puts can be used as insurance against the price of stock you hold falling. If you bought some shares of a stock and they went up in price, by purchasing a put option on the stock at the new price you have in effect locked in the price rise of the shares.

Put options provide owners the right, however, not the obligation, to purchase a specified ⬜uantity of an underlying asset at a given price inside a specified timeframe.

Put options can be found on an array of assets, including securities, indexes, goods, and currencies.

Put option costs are influenced by the underlying property price and period decay.

JUST HOW DO PUT OPTIONS FUNCTION?

A put option gets more valuable as the price of the actual stock depreciates compared to the strike selling price. Conversely, a put option manages to lose its value because the price of the underlying stock raises. Because put options essentially give a short position within the underlying asset, they're useful for hedging purposes or even to speculate on downside price tag action. A defensive put can be used to make sure that losses within the underlying asset do not exceed a Quantity, namely the strike price.

In general, the worth of a put option reduces as its time to expiration approaches because of time decay, as the possibility of the stock dropping below the given strike price lowers. When an option loses its moment price, the intrinsic worth is left, which is equal to the difference between your strike price tag less the actual stock price tag. If a option has intrinsic value, it is in the money (ITM).

From the money (OTM) put options haven't any intrinsic benefit because there will be no advantage of exercising the option. Investors could Quick sell the inventory at the existing higher selling price, rather than trading a from the money put option at an unhealthy strike price.

Time worth, or extrinsic worth, is reflected within the premium of the option. If the strike value of a put option is $20, and the underlying share is currently trading at $19, there's $1 of intrinsic benefit in the option. But the put option may swap for $1.35. The excess $0.35 is definitely time value because the underlying stock value could change prior to when the option expires.

Alternatives to Performing a Put Option

The put owner, referred to as the "writer", doesn't need to hold a option until expiration, and neither will the option shopper. As the root stock price change, the value of the decision changes to mirror the recent main price movements. The option buyer can market their option anytime, either to lower their damage and recoup area of the prime (if OTM), or secure an income (if ITM).

Similarly, the option writer can perform a similar thing. In the event, the underlying stock's price is above the strike price, they could do nothing as the option may expire worthless, plus they can keep the complete premium. If the underlying stock's price is approaching or shedding below the strike price, in order to avoid a significant reduction the option trader may simply choose the option back, obtaining them from the position. The loss or profit is the variation between the premium collected and premium paid to obtain from the position.

Real World Types of Put Options

Assume an entrepreneur owns one put option in the SPDR S&P 500 ETF (SPY)--currently trading at $277.00--with a strike cost of $260 expiring in a single month. Because of this option, they pay a premium of $0.72, or $72 ($0.72 x 100 gives).

The investor gets the right to purchase 100 shares of SPY at a cost of $260 before the expiration date in a single month, that is usually the 3rd Friday from the month, though it could be weekly.

If shares of SPY slide to $250 and the investor exercises the option, the buyer could buy 100 shares of SPY for $250 on the market and promote the shares for the option's writer for $260 each. Therefore, the trader would create $1,000 (100 x ($260-$250)) for the put alternative, less the $72 price they paid for the option. Total profit is $1,000 - $72 = $928, less any commission charges. The maximum damage on the investor is limited for the premium compensated, or $72. The maximum profit is achieved if SPY falls to $0.

Contrary to a extended put option, a brief or written put option obligates an investor to take or purchase shares, of the root stock.

Assume a trader is bullish on SPY, that is currently investing at $277, and does not believe it'll tumble below $260 on the next 8 weeks. The buyer could collect a premium of $0.72 (x 100 stocks) by writing one put contract on SPY, which has a strike cost of $260.

The option writer would collect a complete of $72 ($0.72 x 100). If SPY remains above the $260 strike price, the trader would keep the premium collected because the option would expire from the money and become worthless. This is actually the maximum profit within the market: $72, or the top premium collected.

Conversely, if SPY drops below $260, the investor is on for the hook for buying 100 shares at $260, even though the price may fall to $250, or $200, or lower. Regardless of what price the stock arrives, the put option writer is likely purchasing shares at $260, signifying they experience theoretical threat of $260 per share or $26,000 per deal ($260 x 100 stocks) in the event the underlying stock falls to zero.

Example Study: Buying a Put Option on a House

We have a house that is currently selling for $100,000.

We think that house prices may fall but do not want to sell the house this month. We approach a purchaser with a Contract (proposal).

Our Contract states that we will give the purchaser $1000 for the option (the right but not the obligation) to sell the house at the list price of $100,000.

The contract is valid for 30 days. If we do not sell the house within that period, the purchaser will keep the $1000, and there is no further commitment on either of our behalf.

We have, in fact, purchased the equivalent of a one month put option on the property.

o If the housing market soars in the next 30 days and the house is now valued at $110,000, we let our option expire worthless, and we can sell the house for $110,000.

$110,000 (Current Value) - $1000 (Option Price) - $100,000 (Initial Price) = $9000 (Our Profits).

o If the housing market crashes in the next 30 days and the house is now valued at $90,000, we can exercise our option and sell the house for $100,000.

$100,000 (Sale Price) - $1000 (Option Price) - $90,000 (Current Value) = $9000 (Our locked in value)

CHAPTER 1

THE BASICS OF OPTIONS TRADING PROFITABILITY

Options dealers can benefit by being an option purchaser or an option author. Options take into account potential benefit during both unstable occasions, and when the market is calm or less erratic. This is conceivable because the costs of assets like stocks, currencies, and wares are continually moving, and regardless of what the economic situations are, there is an options methodology that can exploit it.

Options contracts and systems utilizing them have characterized benefit and misfortune, profit, and losses profiles for seeing how much cash you will make or lose.

The maximum benefit you can get from selling an option is the cost of the premium gathered, however, regularly there is boundless drawback potential.

When you buy an option, your upside can be boundless, and the most you can lose is the expense of the options premium.

Contingent upon the options methodology utilized, an individual stands to benefit from any number of economic situations from bull and bear to sideways movements.

Options spreads, in general, top both potential benefits just as misfortunes.

Essentials of Option Profitability

A call option purchaser stands to make a benefit if the fundamental asset, suppose a stock, transcends the strike cost before expiry. A put option purchaser makes a benefit if the value falls beneath the strike cost before the expiration. The definite measure of benefit relies upon the distinction between the stock cost and the option strike cost toward the end or when the option position ends.

A call option writer stands to make a benefit if the basic stock remains underneath the strike cost. When writing a put option, the merchant can only benefit if the value stays over the strike cost. An option author's benefit is constrained to the premium they get for writing the option, which is the option purchaser's expense. Option writers are additionally called option merchants.

Option Buying versus Writing

A option purchaser can make a generous quantifiable profit if the options exchange works out. This is because a stock cost can move altogether past the strike cost.

A option writer makes a relatively smaller return if the option exchange is gainful. This is because the writer's profit is constrained to the premium, regardless of how much the stock moves. So why compose options if the risks are typically overwhelmingly on the option author? A examination in the late 1990s, by the Chicago Mercantile Exchange (CME), found that somewhat over 75% of all options held to expiration lapsed uselessly.

This examination excludes options that were finished off or practiced before expiration. All things being e☐ual, for each option contract that was in the money(ITM) at shutting, there were three that were out of the money (OTM) and, in this way, useless is a ☐uite important measurement.

Evaluating Risk Tolerance

Here's a simple test to assess your risk tolerance to decide if you are in an ideal situation being an option purchaser or an option author. Suppose you can purchase or compose 10 call option contracts, with the cost of each call at $0.50. Each agreement typically has 100 offers as the fundamental asset, so 10 contracts would cost $500 ($0.50 x 100 x 10 contracts).

If you purchase 10 call option contracts, you pay $500, and that is the most extreme misfortune that you can incur. In any case, your potential benefit is theoretically boundless. So what's the trick? The probability of the exchange being gainful isn't high. While this likelihood relies upon the inferred unpredictability of the call option and the timeframe staying to expiration, suppose it 25%.

Then again, if you compose 10 call option contracts, your most extreme benefit is the measure of the superior premium, or $500, while your losses are theoretically boundless. Be that as it may, the chances of the options exchange being gainful are primarily to support you, at 75%.

So would you risk $500, realizing that you have a 75% shot of losing your venture and a 25% possibility of making a benefit? Or then again would you want to make a limit of $500, realizing that you have a 75% shot of keeping the whole sum or part of it, yet have a 25% possibility of the exchange being a losing one?

The response to those inquiries will give you an idea of your risk resilience and whether you are in a ideal situation being an option purchaser or option author.

It is imperative to remember that these are the general measurements that apply to all options, yet on specific occasions, it might be progressively advantageous to be an option writer or a purchaser in a particular asset. Utilizing the correct strategy at the perfect time could change these chances altogether.

Option Strategies Risk/Reward

While calls and puts can be joined in different changes to frame complex options techniques, how about we assess the risk/reward of the four most essential strategies.

Buying a Call

This is the essential option strategy. It is a moderately okay strategy because the most considerable loss is confined to the premium paid to purchase the call, while the most extreme reward is possibly boundless. Although, as expressed prior, the chances of the exchange being entirely beneficial are typically genuinely low. "This "generally safe" strategy expects that the complete expense of the option speaks to a little level of the investor's capital. Risking all capital on a solitary call option would make it a risky exchange because all the cash could be lost if the option terminates useless.

Buying a Put

This is another strategy that is generally okay, yet has conceivably high compensation if the exchange works out. Buying puts is a practical option in contrast to the riskier strategy of short selling the fundamental asset. Puts can likewise be purchased to support drawback risk in a portfolio. But because value records typically pattern higher after some time, which implies that stocks by and large will in general advance more fre□uently than they decay, the risk/remunerate profile of the put purchaser is marginally less ideal than that of a call purchaser.

Writing a Put

Put writing is a favored strategy of cutting edge options brokers because, in the direst outcome imaginable, the stock is appointed to the put author (they need to purchase the stock), while the most ideal situation is that the writer holds everything of the option premium. The greatest risk of put writing is that the author may wind up paying a lot for a stock on the off-chance that it tanks. The risk/remunerate profile of put writing is more ominous than that of put or call buying because the most extreme reward rises to the premium got, yet the greatest misfortune is a lot higher. All things considered, as talked about previously, the likelihood of having the option to make a benefit is higher.

Writing a Call

Call writing comes in two structures, secured and stripped. Secured call writing is another most loved strategy of middle of the road to cutting edge option dealers, and is commonly used to create additional revenues from a portfolio. It includes writing calls on stocks held inside the portfolio. Revealed or stripped call writing is the select area of risk-tolerant, sophisticated options merchants, as it has a risk profile like that of a short deal in stock. The most extreme reward in call writing is equivalent to the premium gotten. The greatest risk with a secured call strategy is that the basic stock will be "called away." With exposed call writing, the most extreme misfortune is theoretically boundless, similarly, for what it's worth, with a short deal.

Options Spreads

As a rule, brokers or investors will join options utilizing a spread strategy, buying at least one option to sell at least one distinct asset. Spreading will balance the premium paid on the grounds that the sold option premium will net against the options premium bought. The risk and return profiles of a spread will top out the potential benefit or misfortune. Spreads can be made to exploit almost any foreseen value activity and can run from the easy to the complex. Similarly, as with individual options, any spread strategy can be either purchased or sold.

Credit Spread And Debit Spread: The Difference?

During trading or investing in options, there are several option spread strategies that one could employ—a spread being the purchase and sale of different options on the same underlying as a package.

While we can classify spreads in various ways, one standard feature is whether the strategy is a credit spread or a debit spread. Credit spreads, or net credit spreads, are spread strategies that involve net receipts of premiums, whereas debit spreads include net payments of premiums.

A option spread is a strategy that involves the simultaneous buying and selling of options on the same underlying asset.

A credit spread includes selling a high-premium option while obtaining a low-premium option in a similar class or related security, bringing about credit to the merchant's record.

A charge spread includes buying a high-premium option while selling a low-premium option in a similar class or related security, bringing about a charge from the broker's record.

Credit Spreads

A credit spread includes selling, or writing, a high-premium option, and at the same time buying a lower premium option. The premium received from the composed option is higher than the premium paid for the long option, bringing about a credit to the merchant or investor's record when the position is opened. Whenever merchants or investors utilize a credit spread strategy, the most extreme benefit they get is the net premium. The credit spread results in a profit that is limited by the options' spreads. For instance, a broker actualizes a credit spread strategy by writing one March call option with a strike cost of $30 for $3 and buying one March call option at $40 for $1. Because the typical multiplier on a value option is 100, the net premium received is $200 for the exchange. Moreover, the merchant will benefit if the spread strategy limits.

A bearish trader expects stock prices to decrease, and, therefore, buys call options (long call) at a specific strike price and sells (short call) the same number of call options within the same class and with the same expiration at a lower strike price. In contrast, bullish traders expect stock prices to rise, and therefore, buy call options at a certain strike price and sell the same number of call options within the same class and with the same expiration at a higher strike price.

Debit Spreads

Conversely, a debit spread—most often used by beginners to options strategies—involves buying an option with a higher premium and simultaneously selling an option with a lower premium, where the premium paid for the long option of the spread is more than the premium received from the written option.

Unlike a credit spread, a debit spread results in a premium debited, or paid, from the trader's or investor's account when the position is opened. Debit spreads are primarily used to offset the costs associated with owning long options positions.

For example, a trader buys one May put option with a strike price of $20 for $5 and simultaneously sells one May put option with a strike price of $10 for $1. Therefore, he paid $4, or $400 for the trade. If the trade is out of the money, his max loss is reduced to $400, as opposed to $500 if he only bought the put option.

Straddle

A straddle is a neutral options strategy that involves simultaneously buying both a put option and a call option for the same underlying security with the same strike price and the same expiration date.

A trader will profit from a long straddle when the price of the security rises or falls from the strike price by an amount more than the total cost of the premium paid. The profit potential is virtually unlimited, so long as the price of the underlying security moves very sharply.

A straddle implies what the expected volatility and trading range of security may be by the expiration date.

Understanding Straddles

More broadly, straddle strategies in finance refer to two separate transactions which both involve the same underlying security, with the two-component transactions offsetting one another. Investors tend to employ a straddle when they anticipate a significant move in a stock's price but are unsure about whether the price will move up or down.

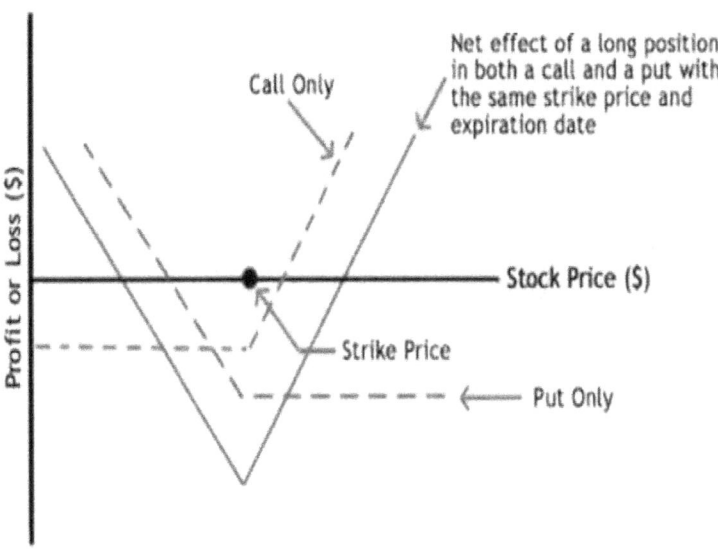

A straddle can give a broker two noteworthy intimations about what the options market thinks about a stock. First is the unpredictability the market is anticipating from the security. Second is the standard trading scope of the stock by the expiration date.

Putting Together a Straddle

To decide the expense of making a straddle, one must include the cost of the put and the call together. For instance, if a dealer accepts that a stock may rise or tumble from its present cost of $55 following income on March 1, they could make a straddle. The merchant would hope to buy one put and one call at the $55 strike with an expiration date of March 15. To decide the expense of making the straddle, the broker would include the cost of one March 15 $55 call and one March 15 $55 put. In the event that both the calls and the puts exchange for $2.50 each, the total cost or premium paid would be $5.00 for the two contracts.

The premium paid proposes that the stock would need to rise or fall by 9% from the $55 strike cost to gain a benefit by March 15. The sum the stock is expected to rise-or-fall is a proportion of the future anticipated unpredictability of the stock. To decide how much the stock needs to rise or fall, divide the premium paid by the strike value, which is $5/$55, or 9%.

Finding the Trading Range

To decide the normal trading range of the stock, one would include or subtract the $5 premium to or from the $55 strike cost. For this situation, it makes a trading range of $50 to $60. In the event that the stock exchanged inside the zone of $50 to $60, the merchant would lose a portion of their cash; however, not every last bit of it. It is conceivable to acquire a benefit if the stock ascents or falls outside of the $50 to $60 zone.

Winning a Profit

In the event that the stock tumbled to $48, the calls would be worth $0, while the puts would be worth $7 at expiration. That would convey a benefit of $2 to the merchant. Be that as it may, if the stock went to $57, the calls would be worth $2, and the puts would be worth zero, resulting in a loss to the dealer of $3. The most desired outcome could be derived if the stock value remains at or close to the strike cost.

True Example

The options market was inferring that AMD's stock could rise or fall 20% from the $26 strike cost at 06,10,2018 for expiration on November 16, because it cost $5.10 to get one put and call. It put the stock in a trading scope of $20.90 to $31.15. After seven days, the detailed organization outcomes and offers dove from $22.70 to $19.27 on October 25. For this situation, the dealer would have earned a benefit because the stock fell outside of the range, surpassing the premium expense of buying the puts and calls.

Strike Price

A strike cost is the set cost at which a derivative contract can be purchased or sold when it is worked out. For call options, the strike cost is the place the option holder can purchase the security; for put options, the strike cost is the cost at which the security can be sold.

Strike cost is otherwise called the activity cost.

Derivatives are monetary items whose value is based (inferred) on the hidden asset, typically another money related instrument.

The strike cost, otherwise called the activity cost, is the most significant determinant of option value.

Understanding Strike Prices

Strike costs are utilized in derivatives (for the most part options) trading. Derivatives are monetary items whose value is based on, or determined by, the fundamental asset, typically another money-related instrument. The strike cost is a key variable of call and put options. For instance, the purchaser of a stock option call would have the right, yet not the commitment, to purchase that stock in the future at the strike cost. Thus, the purchaser of a stock option put would have the right, yet not the commitment, to sell that stock in the future at the strike cost.

The strike or, on the other hand, exercise cost is the most significant determinant of option value. Strike costs are built in when an agreement is first composed. It tells the investor what value the basic asset must reach before the option is in-the-money (ITM). Strike costs are standardized, which means they are at fixed dollar sums, for example, $31, $32, $33, $102.50, $105, etc.

The value distinction between the hidden stock cost and the strike cost decides an option's value. For purchasers of a call option, if the strike cost is over the unknown stock value, the option is out of the money (OTM). For this situation, the option doesn't have inherent value; however, it might, in any case, have a value dependent on instability and time until expiration as both of these two components could put the option in cash in the future. Alternately, if the hidden stock cost is over the strike value, the option will have inherent value and be in cash.

A purchaser of a put option will be in the money when the basic stock cost is beneath the strike cost and be out of the money when the hidden stock cost is over the strike cost. Once more, an OTM option won't have inherent value, yet it might, in any case, have a value dependent on the unpredictability of the hidden asset and the time left until option expiration.

Strike Price Example

Suppose there are two option contracts. One is a call option with a $100 strike cost. The other is a call option with a $150 strike cost. The present cost of the hidden stock is $145. Both call options are equivalent; the main contrast is the strike cost.

At expiration, the principal contract is worth $45. That is, it is in cash by $45. This is on the grounds that the stock is trading $45 higher than the strike cost.

The subsequent contract is out of the cash by $5. On the off chance that the cost of the hidden asset is underneath the call's strike cost at expiration, the option expires useless.

If we have two put options, both going to lapse, and one has a strike cost of $40 and the other has a strike cost of $50, we can look to the present stock cost to see which option has value. If the basic stock is trading at $45, the $50 put option has a $5 value. This is on the grounds that the hidden stock price is beneath the strike cost of the put.

The $40 put option has no value, because the basic stock price is over the strike cost. Recall that put options enable the option purchaser to sell at the strike cost. There is no point utilizing the option to sell at $40 when they can sell at $45 in the stock market. In this manner, the $40 strike value put is useless at expiration.

Expiration Date? (Derivatives)

An expiration date in derivatives is the latest day that derivative contracts, for example, options or futures, are substantial. At the latest on this day, investors will have officially chosen how to manage their lapsing position. After that time, the agreement has lapsed.

Before an option terminates, its proprietors can practice the option, close the situation to understand their benefit or losses, or let the agreement lapse useless.

Contingent upon the kind of derivative, the expiration date can bring about different results.

Option proprietors can practice the option, and acknowledge benefits or misfortunes, or let it lapse useless.

Futures contract proprietors can move over the agreement to a future date, or close their position and take conveyance of the asset or item.

Essentials of Expiration Dates

Expiration dates, and what they speak to, shift dependent on the derivative being exchanged. The expiration date for recorded stock options in the United States is regularly the third Friday of the agreement month or the month that the agreement terminates. On months that the Friday falls on a vacation, the expiration date is on a Thursday preceding the third Friday. When an options or futures contract passes its expiration date, the agreement is invalid. The final day to exchange value options is the Friday preceding expiry. Merchants must choose how to manage their options by this last trading day.

A few options have a programmed exercise arrangement. These options are automatically practiced in the event that they are on the money(OTM) at the hour of expiry. On the off chance that a broker doesn't need the option to be worked out, they should finish off or roll the situation by the last trading day.

Record options additionally terminate on the third Friday of the month, and this is likewise the last trading day for American style list options. For European style record options, the last trading day is typically the day preceding expiration.

Expiration and Option Value

When all is said in done, the longer an option has remaining to expiration, the more time it has to arrive at its strike cost and, in this way, the extra time value it has.

There are two sorts of options, calls and puts. Calls give the holder the right, however not the commitment, to purchase a stock if it arrives at a specific strike cost by the expiration date. Puts give the holder the right, yet not the commitment, to sell a stock if it arrives at a specific strike cost by the expiration date.

This is the reason the expiration date is so critical to options merchants. The idea of time is at the core of what gives options their value. After the put or call lapses, time value doesn't exist. At the end of the day, when the derivative terminates, the investor doesn't hold any rights that accompany owning the call or put.

NOTE: The expiration time of an options contract is the date and time when it is rendered invalid and void. It is more explicit than the expiration date and ought not to be mistaken for the last time to exchange that option.

Expiration and Futures Value

Futures are not quite the same as options in that even an out of the cash futures contract (losing position) holds value after expiry. For instance, an oil contract speaks to barrels of oil. If a dealer retains that agreement until expiry, it is on the grounds that they either need to purchase (they purchased the agreement) or sell (they sold the agreement) the oil that the agreement speaks to. Subsequently, the futures contract doesn't terminate uselessly, and the gatherings included are subject to one another to satisfy their part of the arrangement. Those that don't have any desire or obligation to fulfill the contract must roll or close their situations, at the latest, on the last trading day.

Futures dealers holding the terminating contract should close it at the very latest expiration, regularly called the "last trading day", to understand their benefit or misfortune. On the other hand, they can hold the agreement and request that their merchant purchase or sell the basic asset to which the agreement speaks. Retail dealers don't typically do this; however, organizations do. For instance, an oil maker utilizing futures contracts to sell oil can sell their tanker. Futures brokers can likewise "roll" their position. This is an end to their present exchange, and a prompt reinstitution of the exchange of an agreement that is farther from expiry.

Strangle

A strangle is an options strategy where the investor holds a situation in both a call and a put option with various strike costs, however with a similar expiration date and basic asset. A strangle is a decent strategy if you figure the hidden security will encounter an enormous value development sooner rather than later yet are uncertain of the course. In any case, it is productive for the most part if the asset swings solidly in cost.

A strangle is like a straddle, yet utilizes options at various strike costs, while a straddle utilizes a call and put at a similar strike cost.

A strangle is gainful if the hidden asset swings firmly in cost.

How Does a Strangle Work?

Strangles come in two structures:

In a long strangle—the more typical strategy—the investor at the same time purchases an out-of-the-cash call and an out-of-the-cash put option. The call option's strike cost is higher than the basic asset's present market cost, while the put has a strike value that is lower than the asset's market cost. This strategy has huge benefit potential since the call option has theoretically significant upside if the basic asset ascends in cost, while the put option can benefit if the basic asset falls. The risk on the exchange is constrained to the premium paid for the two options.

A investor doing a short strangle sells a out-of-the-cash put and an out-of-the-cash call. This methodology is an unbiased strategy with restricted benefit potential. A short strangle benefits when the cost of the hidden stock exchanges a thin extend between the breakeven focuses. The most extreme benefit is comparable to the net premium received for writing the two options, less trading expenses.

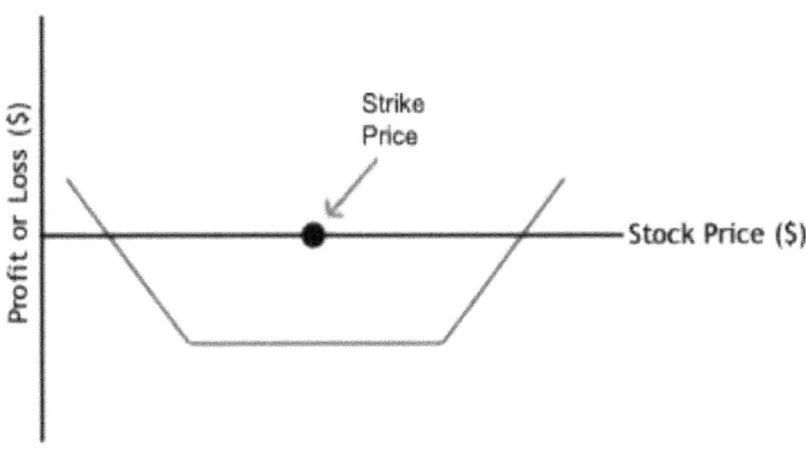

A Strangle vs a Straddle

Strangles and straddles are comparative options strategies that enable investors to benefit from enormous moves to the upside or drawback. Nonetheless, a long straddle includes buying at the money call and put options—where the strike cost is indistinguishable from the basic asset's market cost—as opposed to out-of-the-money options. A short straddle is like a short strangle, with constrained benefit potential that is identical to the premium gathered from writing the at-the-money call and put options.

With the straddle, the investor benefits when the cost of the security rises or tumbles from the strike cost by a sum more than the complete expense of the premium. So, it doesn't require as enormous a value bounce. Buying a strangle is commonly more affordable than a straddle; however, it conveys more serious risk in that the basic asset needs to make a greater move to produce a benefit.

Pros

Advantages from asset's value move in either course.

Less expensive than different options methodologies, similar to straddles.

Boundless benefit potential.

Cons

Requires a huge change in asset's cost.

May convey more risk than different methodologies.

Example of a Strangle

To illustrate, suppose that Starbucks (SBUX) is right now trading at US$50 per share. To utilize the strangle option strategy, a merchant goes into two option positions, one call and one put. The call has a strike of $52, and the premium is $3, for a complete expense of $300 ($3 x 100 offers). The put option has a strike cost of $48, and the premium is $2.85, for a complete expense of $285 ($2.85 x 100 offers). The two options have a similar expiration date.

In the event, that the cost of the stock remains somewhere in the range of $48 and $52 over the life of the option, the misfortune to the dealer will be $585, which is the all-out expense of the two option contracts ($300 + $285).

Alternatively, suppose Starbucks' stock encounters some volatility. In the event that the cost of the shares winds up at $40, the call option will terminate uselessly, and the loss will be $300 for that option. Be that as it may, the put option has picked up value and will deliver a benefit of $715 ($1,000 less the underlying option cost of $285) for that option. Subsequently, the all-out profit to the merchant is $415 ($715 benefit - $300 misfortune).

In the event that the value ascends to $55, the put option lapses useless and brings about a loss of $285. The call option gets a benefit of $200 ($500 value - $300 cost). When the misfortune from the put option is figured in, the exchange results in a loss of $85 ($200 benefit - $285) in light of the fact that the value move wasn't huge enough to make up for the expense of the options. The employable idea is the move being huge enough. On the off chance that Starbucks had risen $10 in cost, to $60 per share, the absolute addition would have again been $415 ($1000 value - $300 for call option premium - $285 for a lapsed put option).

Option Premium

An option premium is the present market cost of an option contract. It is the revenue received by the merchant (author) of an option contract. In-the-money option premiums are made out of two elements: natural and outward value. Out-of-the-money options' premiums comprise exclusively of extraneous value.

For stock options, the premium is cited as a dollar sum for each offer, and most contracts speak to the responsibility of 100 offers.

The premium on a option is its cost in the market.

Option premiums consist of outward, or time value, for out-of-the-money contracts, and both inherent and extraneous value for in-the-money options.

A option's top-notch will by and large be more noteworthy given more time to expiration and additionally more prominent inferred volatility.

Understanding Option Premium

Investors who compose, or intend to sell for this situation, calls or puts use option premiums as a wellspring of current pay in accordance with a more extensive venture strategy to fence all or a part of a portfolio. Option costs cited on a trade, for example, the Chicago Board Options Exchange (CBOE), are considered premiums when in doubt, on the grounds that the options themselves have no fundamental value.

The segments of an option premium incorporate its natural value, its time value, and the inferred volatility of the basic asset. The nearer the expiration date of the option draws, the time value will edge consistently closer to $0, while the natural value will intently speak to the distinction between the fundamental security's cost and the strike cost of the agreement.

Elements of Option Premium

The fundamental variables influencing an option's cost are the basic security's cost, moneyness, valuable existence of the option, and inferred volatility. As the cost of the basic security changes, the option premium changes. As the fundamental security's cost builds, the premium of a call option increases, yet the premium of a put option diminishes. As the fundamental security's cost decreases, the premium of a put option increases, and the inverse are valid for call options.

The moneyness influences the option's premium because it shows the distance away the basic security cost is from the predefined strike cost. As an option turns out to be further in-the-money, the option's premium ordinarily increases. On the other hand, the option premium reduces as the option turns out to be farther out-of-the-money. For instance, as an option turns out to be farther out-of-the-money, the option premium loses inherent value, and the value stems essentially from the time value.

The time until expiration, or the helpful life, influences the time value portion of the option's premium. As the expiration date nears, the option's top-notch premium stems principally from the natural value. For instance, profound out-of-the-money options that are lapsing in one trading day would regularly be worth $0, or near $0.

Suggested Volatility and Option Price

Suggested volatility is obtained from the option's value, which is connected to an option's evaluating model which demonstrates how unpredictable a stock's cost might be in the future. Additionally, it influences the outward value bit of option premiums. In the event that investors are long options, an expansion in inferred volatility would add to the value. This is because the more prominent the volatility of the fundamental asset, the more shots the option has of completing in-the-money. The inverse is valid whenever inferred volatility diminishes.

For instance, expect an investor is long one call option with an annualized suggested volatility of 20%. In this manner, if the inferred volatility increases to half during the option's life, the call option premium would acknowledge this in its value. A option's vega is its adjustment in premium given a 1% change in inferred volatility.

CHAPTER 2

IN THE MONEY (ITM)

ITM is a term that refers to a option that has inherent value. ITM, in this manner, shows that a option has value in a strike value that is good in contrast to the predominant market cost of the fundamental asset.

An in-the-money call option implies the option holder has the chance to purchase the security beneath its present market cost.

An in-the-money put option implies the option holder can sell the security over its present market cost.

An option that is ITM doesn't really mean the dealer is making a benefit on the exchange. The cost of buying the option and any commission charges should likewise be considered. In-the-money options might have appeared differently in relation to out-of-the-money (OTM) options.

If the market cost is over the strike cost, then we can say a call option is in-the-money.

If the market cost is underneath the strike cost, then we can say a put option is in-the-money.

ITM options contracts tend to have higher premiums than different options that are not ITM.

A Brief Overview

Investors who buy call options are bullish that the asset's cost will increase and close over the strike cost by the option's expiration date. Options are accessible to exchange for some money-related items, for example, bonds and products, at the same time, values are one of the most prominent for investors.

Options give the purchaser a chance, however, not the commitment, of buying or selling the fundamental security at the agreement's expressed strike cost, by the predefined expiration date. The strike cost is the exchange value or execution cost for the portions of the hidden security.

Options accompanies a forthright charge cost, called the exceptional, that investors pay to purchase the agreement. Different elements decide the exceptional's value. These variables incorporate the present market cost of the hidden security, time until the expiration date, and the value of the strike cost in relationship to the security's market cost. Typically, the top-notch demonstrates the value members place on some random option. An option that has value will probably have a higher premium related with it versus one that has minimal possibility of profiting for a investor.

The two segments of an option's premium are natural and outward value. In-the-money options have both characteristic and extraneous value, while out-of-the-money option's premiums contain just outward (time) value.

NOTE: Explaining In The Money Call Options

Call options take into consideration the buying of the basic asset at a given cost before an expressed date. The exceptional becomes possibly the most important factor when deciding if a option is in-the-money or not, yet can be deciphered diversely depending upon the kind of option included. A call option is said to be in-the-money if the stock's present market cost is higher than the option's strike cost. The sum that a option is in-the-money is called the inherent value meaning the option is at any rate worth that sum.

For instance, a call option with a strike of $25 would be in-the-money if the fundamental stock was trading at $30 per share. What separates the strike and the present market cost is typically the measure of the premium for the option. Investors hoping to purchase a specific in-the-money call option will pay the premium or the spread between the strike and the market cost.

In any case, a investor holding a call option that is terminating in-the-money can practice it and gain the difference between the strike cost and market cost. Whether the exchange was gainful or not depends upon the investors all out cost of buying the agreement and any commission to process that exchange.

It is critical to take note that ITM doesn't mean the dealer is profiting. When buying an ITM option, the broker will re uire the option's value to move more distant into the money to make a benefit. As it were, investors buying call options need the stock cost to move sufficiently high with the goal that it, at any rate, takes care of the expense of the option's premium.

Clarifying In-The-Money Put Options

While call options permit the acquisition of an asset, a put option achieves the contrary activity. Investors purchase these options contracts that enable them to sell the basic security at the strike cost when they anticipate that the value of the security should diminish. Put option purchasers are bearish on the development of the hidden security.

An in-the-money put option indicates that the strike cost is over the market cost of the underlying asset. Holding an ITM put option at expiry for an investor implies the stock cost is beneath the strike cost and it's conceivable the option merits working out. A put option purchaser is trusting the stock's cost will fall far enough underneath the option's strike to spread the expense of the premium for buying the put.

The closer the expiration date, the value of the put option will fall in a procedure known as time rot.

Pros

Being in-the-money (ITM) at expiry for a call option holder gets an opportunity to make a benefit if the market cost is over the strike cost.

A investor holding an in-the-money put option gets an opportunity to gain a benefit if the market cost is beneath the strike cost.

Cons

In-the-money options are more costly than different options because investors pay for the benefit previously connected with the agreement.

Investors should likewise consider premium and commission costs to decide benefit from an in-the-money option.

Different Considerations

At the point when the strike cost and market cost of the hidden security are equivalent, the option is called at-the-money (ATM). Options can likewise be out-of-the-money, which means the strike cost isn't great to the market cost. Every OTM call option tends to have a higher strike cost than the market cost of the stock.

On the other hand, an OTM put option would have a lower strike cost than the market cost. An OTM option implies that the option still can't seem to profit on the grounds that the stock's rise hasn't moved enough to make the option productive. Accordingly, OTM options, for the most part, have lower premiums than ITM options.

In short, the measure of premium paid for an option depends largely on the degree a option is ITM, ATM, or OTM. Be that as it may, numerous different variables can influence the premium of an option, including how much the stock vacillates, called volatility, and the time until the expiration.

Genuine Example of ITM Options

Let's say an investor operates a call option on Bank of America (BAC) stock with a strike cost of $30. The offers right now exchange at $33, making the agreement in-the-money. The call option enables the investor to purchase the stock for $30, and they could promptly sell the stock for $33, giving them a $3 per share contrast. Every option contract speaks to 100 offers, so the inherent value is $3 x 100 = $300.

On the off chance that the investor paid a premium of $3.50 for the call, they would not benefit from the exchange. He would have paid $350 ($3.50 x 100 = $350) while just picking up $300 on the contrast between the strike cost and market cost. As it were, he'd lose $50 on the exchange. Be that as it may, the option is considered ITM in light of the fact that, at expiry, the option will have a value of $3 despite the fact that he's not winning a benefit.

Additionally, if the stock value tumbled from $33 to $29, the $30 strike value call is no longer ITM. It would be $1 OTM. It's essential to take note that while the strike cost is fixed, the cost of the hidden asset will vacillate influencing the degree to which the option is in-the-money. An ITM option can move to ATM or even OTM before its expiration date.

CHAPTER 3

OUT OF THE MONEY (OTM)

This(OTM) is a term used to depict an option contract that just contains inborn value. These options will have a delta under 50.0.

Every OTM call option always has a strike value that is higher than the market cost of the hidden asset. On the other hand, an OTM put option has a strike value that is lower than the market cost of the hidden asset.

OTM options might be stood out from in-the-money (ITM) options.

Out-of-the-money implies an option has no natural value, just extraneous value.

A call option is OTM if the hidden's cost is underneath the strike cost. A put option is OTM if the hidden's cost is over the strike cost.

An option can likewise be in-the-money or at-the-money.

OTM options are more affordable than ITM or ATM options. This is because ITM options have inborn value, and ATM options are near having inherent value.

Option Basics

For a top-notch, stock options give the buyer the right, however not the commitment, to purchase or sell the hidden stock at a settled upon cost, known as the strike cost, before a settled upon date, known as the expiration date.

An option to purchase a basic asset is a call option, while an option to sell a hidden asset is a put option. A merchant may buy a call option in the event that they expect the basic asset's cost to surpass the strike cost before the expiration date. Alternately, a put option empowers the broker to benefit on a decrease in the asset's cost. Because they get their value from that of fundamental security, options are derivatives.

An option can be OTM, ITM, or at-the-money (ATM). An ATM option is one where the strike cost and cost of the hidden are equivalent.

Out-of-the-Money Options

By figuring out where the present cost of the hidden is in connection to the strike cost of that option, you can tell if an option is out-of-the-money. For a call option, if the fundamental cost is beneath the strike value, that option is OTM. For a put option, if the hidden's cost is over the strike value, at that point that option is OTM. OTM option has no natural value, yet just has outward or time value.

However, because it's out-of-the-money doesn't mean a merchant can't make a benefit on that option. Every option has an expense, called the premium. A broker could have purchased an out-of-the-money option, yet the option is drawing nearer to being in-the-money (ITM). That option could wind up being worth more than the merchant paid for the option, despite the fact that it is right now out-of-the-money. At expiry, however, an option is useless in the event that it is OTM. In a this manner, if a option is OTM, the dealer should sell it preceding expiry so as to recover any extraneous value that is perhaps remaining.

Using a stock that is trading at $10, for example, call options with strike costs above $10 would be OTM calls, while put options with strike costs underneath $10 would be OTM puts.

NOTE: OTM options are not worth working out, on the grounds that the present market is offering an exchange level more engaging than the option's strike cost.

Out-of-the-Money Options Example

A merchant needs to purchase a call option on Vodafone stock. They pick a call option with a $20 strike cost. The option terminates in five months and expenses $0.50. This gives them the privilege to purchase 100 portions of the stock before the option terminates. The all-out expense of the option is $50 (100 offers * $0.50), in addition to an exchange commission. The stock is at present trading at $18.50.

After buying the option, there is no motivation to practice it in light of the fact that by practicing the option they need to pay $20 for the stock when they can as of now get it at a market cost of $18.50.

This option is OTM, yet that doesn't mean it is useless yet. The dealer simply paid $0.50 for the potential that the stock will rise above $20 inside the following five months.

On the off chance that the option is OTM at expiry it is useless, but preceding expiry, that option will, in any case, have some extraneous value which is reflected in the premium or cost of the option. The cost of the hidden may never reach $20; however, the premium of the option may increment to $0.75 or $1 in the event that it draws near. Along these lines, the broker could even now harvest a benefit on the out-of-the-money option itself by selling it at a higher premium than they paid for it.

However, if the stock value moves to $22—the option is presently ITM—it merits practicing the option. The option gives them the privilege to purchase at $20, and the present market cost is $22. The contrast between the strike cost and the present market cost is known as a natural value, which is $2.

For this situation, our merchant winds up with a net benefit or advantage. The option they paid $0.50 for is currently worth $2. The net $1.50 is benefit or preferred position.

Yet, imagine a scenario where the stock possibly encouraged to $20.25 when the option terminated. For this situation, the option is still ITM, yet the merchant really lost money. They paid $0.50 for the option; however, the option just has $0.25 of value currently, bringing about a lost $0.25 ($0.50 - $0.25).

Implied volatility

Implied volatility is a metric that catches the market's perspective on the probability of changes in a given security's cost. Investors can utilize it to extend future moves and market interest, and frequently use it to value options contracts.

Implied volatility isn't equivalent to verifiable volatility, otherwise called acknowledged volatility or factual volatility. The verifiable volatility figure will quantify past market changes and their real outcomes.

Implied volatility is the market's estimate of future development in a security's cost.

Implied volatility is regularly used to value options contracts. High implied volatility brings about options with higher premiums and the other way around.

Supply versus re%uest and time value are major deciding variables for figuring implied volatility.

Implied volatility increases in bearish markets and diminishes when the market is bullish.

Comprehension Implied Volatility

Implied volatility is the market's estimate of future development in a security's cost. It is a measurement utilized by investors to assess future changes (volatility) of a security's cost dependent on certain prescient components. Implied volatility, indicated by the image σ (sigma), can frequently be believed to be an indicator of market risk. It is usually communicated utilizing rates and standard deviations over a predefined time period.

When applied to the stock market, implied volatility for the most part increases in bearish markets, when investors accept value costs will decay after some time. IV diminishes when the market is bullish, and investors agree that costs will ascend after some time. Bearish markets are viewed as unfortunate, and conse%uently riskier, to most of the value investors.

Implied volatility doesn't anticipate the heading where the value change will continue. For instance, high volatility implies an enormous value swing, yet the cost could swing upward—extremely high—descending—exceptionally low—or vary between the two headings. Low volatility implies that the value likely won't make vast, erratic changes.

Implied Volatility and Options

Implied volatility is one of the integral factors in the evaluating of options. Buying options contracts let the holder purchase or sell an asset at a particular cost during a pre-decided period. It approximates the future value of the option, and the option's present value is additionally contemplated. Options that posses high implied volatility will have higher premiums and the other way around.

It is imperative to recollect that implied volatility depends on likelihood. It is just a gauge of future costs as opposed to a sign of them. Although investors consider implied volatility when settling on venture options, and this reliance unavoidably has some effect on the costs themselves.

There is no certification that an option's cost will pursue the anticipated example. However, when thinking about speculation, it helps to consider the moves different investors are making with the option, and implied volatility is legitimately associated with the market conclusion, which thus influences option evaluating.

Implied volatility likewise influences the evaluating of non-option budgetary instruments, for example, a loan cost top, which confines the sum a financing cost on an item can be raised.

Option Pricing Models and IV

Implied volatility can be controlled by utilizing an option evaluating model. It is the main factor in the model that isn't straightforwardly discernible in the market. Rather, the scientific option valuing model uses different components to decide implied volatility and the option's premium.

The Black-Scholes Model, a broadly utilized and surely understood options estimating model, factors in current stock value, options strike value, time until expiration (signified as a percent of a year), and no-risk financing costs. The Black-Scholes Model is brisk in figuring any number of option costs. In any case, it can't precisely ascertain American options, because it just considers the cost at an option's expiration date. American options are those that the proprietor may practice whenever up to and including the expiration day.

The Binomial Model utilizes a tree outline with volatility calculated in at each level, to demonstrate every conceivable way an option's cost can take, and works in reverse to decide one cost. The best part of this model is the fact that you can return to it anytime for the plausibility of early work out. Early trade is executing the agreement's activities at its strike cost before the agreement's expiration. Early practice occurs in American style options. In any case, the computations engaged with this model set aside a long effort to decide, so this model isn't the best in hurried circumstances.

Components Affecting Implied Volatility

Similarly, likewise, with the market in general, implied volatility is dependent upon eccentric changes. Market interest are major deciding elements for implied volatility. At the point when an asset is in extreme interest, the value will increase generally. So does the implied volatility, which prompts a higher option premium because of the risky idea of the option.

The inverse is likewise valid. At the point when there is a lot of inventory yet insufficient market request, the implied volatility falls, and the option cost ends up less expensive.

Another premium impacting element is the time value of the option, or the measure of time until the option lapses. A short-dated option regularly brings about low implied volatility, though a long-dated option, will, in general, bring about high implied volatility. The distinction lies in the measure of time left before the expiration of the agreement. Because there is a lengthier time, the cost has an all-encompassing period to move into a high-value level as compared to the strike cost.

Advantages and disadvantages of Using Implied Volatility

Implied volatility evaluates showcase notion. It assesses the size of the development an asset may take. Be that as it may, as referenced prior, it doesn't demonstrate the heading of the development. Option scholars will utilize figurings, including implied volatility to value options contracts. Likewise, numerous investors will take a gander at the IV when they pick speculation. During times of high volatility, they may put resources into more secure areas or items.

Implied volatility doesn't have a premise on the essential fundamentals of the market asset, yet depends on exclusively on cost. Additionally, unfriendly news or occasions, for example, wars or cataclysmic events, may affect the implied volatility.

Pros

Evaluates advertised opinion, vulnerability.

Help set options costs.

Decides trading strategy.

Cons

In light of costs, not basics.

Touchy to unforeseen variables, news occasions.

Predicts development, yet not the course.

Genuine Example

Brokers and investors use outlining to break down implied volatility. One particularly prominent instrument is the Chicago Board Options Exchange (CBOE) Volatility Index (VIX). The CBOE's VIX is a continuous market file. The file uses value information from close dated, close to the-money S&P 500 record options to extend desires for volatility throughout the following 30 days.

Investors can utilize the VIX to contrast various protections, or to check the stock market's volatility overall, and structure trading methodologies as needed.

How Options Work

As far as evaluating option contracts, it is basically about deciding the probabilities of future value occasions. For example, a call value goes up as the stock (fundamental) goes up. This is the way to understanding the overall value of options.

The less time there is until expiry, the less value a option will have. This is on the grounds that the odds of a value move in the fundamental stock decrease as we move nearer to expiry. This is the reason an option is a squandering asset. If you purchase a one-month option that is out-of-the-money, and the stock doesn't move, the option turns out to be less significant as time passes. Because time is a part of the cost of an option, a one-month option will be less significant than a three-month option. This is because with additional time accessible, the likelihood of a cost move increases, and the other way around.

In like manner, a similar option strike that lapses in a year will cost more than a similar strike for one month. This squandering highlight of options is a consequence of time rot. A similar option will be more worthless tomorrow than it is today if the cost of the stock doesn't move.

Volatility additionally builds the cost of a option. This is because vulnerability pushes the chances of a result higher. In the event that the volatility of the basic asset increases, bigger cost swings increases the conceivable outcomes of generous moves both here and there. More prominent cost swings will expand the odds of an occasion happening. Along these lines, the more prominent the volatility, the more noteworthy the cost of the option. Options trading and volatility are intrinsically connected to one another along these lines.

Generally, U.S. exchange stock option contract is the option to purchase or sell 100 shares; that is the reason you should multiply the agreement premium by 100 to get the aggregate sum you'll need to spend to purchase the call.

What happen to our option investment

September 1 September 21 Expiry Date

Stock Price $67 $78 $62

Option Price $3.15 $8.25 worthless

Contract Value $315 $825 $0

Paper Gain/Loss $0 $510 -$315

Most of the time, holders take their benefits by trading out (finishing off) their position. This implies option holders sell their options in the market, and writers repurchase their situations to close. As indicated by the CBOE, just about 10% of options are worked out, 60% are exchanged (shut) out, and 30% terminate uselessly.

Fluctuations in option costs can be clarified by inherent value and outward value, which is otherwise called time value. A option's premium is the blend of its natural value and time value. Natural value is the in-the-money measure of an option contract, which, for a call option, is the sum over the strike value that the stock is trading. Time value speaks to the additional value a investor needs to pay for an option over the intrinsic value. This is the extraneous value or time value. Along these lines, the cost of the option in our model can be thought of as the following:

Premium = Intrinsic Value + Time Value

$8.25=$8.00+$0.25

In actuality, options quite often exchange at some level over their inherent value, because the likelihood of an occurrence happening is rare or total zero, regardless of whether it is exceptionally improbable.

Options Expiration & Liquidity

Options can also be classified by their span. Short-term options are those that terminate for the most part inside a year. Long-term options with expirations beyond a year are named long-term value expectation protections or LEAPs. LEAPs are indistinguishable from customary options; they simply have longer spans.

Options can likewise be recognized by when their expiration date falls. Sets of options presently terminate week after week on every Friday, toward the part of the bargain, or even once a day. Record and ETF options, in some cases, offer quarterly expiries.

Options Tables

An ever-increasing number of merchants are discovering option information through online sources. While each source has its very own arrangement for showing the information, the key segments, by and large, incorporate the accompanying factors:

Volume (VLM) basically discloses to you what number of contracts of a specific option were exchanged during the most recent session.

The "offer" cost is the most recent value level at which a market member wishes to purchase a specific option.

The "ask" cost is the most recent cost offered by a market member to sell a specific option.

Implied Bid Volatility (IMPL BID VOL) can be thought of as the future vulnerability of value heading and speed. This value is determined by an option-evaluating model, for example, the Black-Scholes model, and speaks to the degree of expected future volatility dependent on the present cost of the option.

Open Interest (OPTN OP) number shows the complete number of contracts of a specific option that have been opened. Open interest diminishes as open exchanges are shut.

Delta can be described as the chance an option will reach the strike price. For example, a 30-delta option has around a 30% possibility of terminating in-the-money.

Gamma (GMM) is the speed the option is moving in or out-of-the-money. Gamma can likewise be thought of as the development of the delta.

Vega is a Greek value that demonstrates the sum by which the cost of the option would be required to change dependent on a one-point change in implied volatility.

Theta is the Greek value that demonstrates how much value an option will lose with the section of one day's time.

The "strike cost" is the cost at which the purchaser of the option can purchase or sell the fundamental security on the off chance that he/she practices the option.

Motivations to Trade Options

Investors and brokers embrace option trading either to support open situations (for instance, buying puts to fence a long position, or buying calls to support a short position) or to hypothesize on likely value developments of a basic asset.

Speculation

Speculation is a bet on future value bearing. An examiner may think the cost of a stock will go up, maybe dependent on central examination or specialized investigation. An examiner may purchase the stock or purchase a call option on the stock. Guessing with a call option—rather than buying the stock by and large—is alluring to certain merchants because options give influence. An out-of-the-money call option may just cost a couple of dollars or even pennies contrasted with the cost of a $100 stock.

The greatest advantage of utilizing options is that of influence. For instance, say an investor has $900 to use on a specific exchange and wants the most value for the money. The investor is bullish in the short term on XYZ Inc. Suppose XYZ is trading at $90. Our investor can purchase a limit of 10 portions of XYZ. XYZ also has three-month calls accessible with a strike cost of $95 for an expensive $3. Presently, rather than buying the shares, the investor purchases three call option contracts. Buying three call options will cost $900 (3 contracts x 100 offers x $3).

Shortly before the call options lapse, assume XYZ is trading at $103, and the calls are trading at $8, so, all in all, the investor sells the calls. Here's how the arrival on venture piles up for each situation.

Through and through acquisition of XYZ shares at $90: Profit = $13 per share x 10 offers = $130 = 14.4% return ($130/$900).

Acquisition of three $95 call option contracts: Profit = $8 x 100 x 3 contracts = $2,400 short premium paid of $900 = $1500 = 166.7% return ($1,500/$900).

Obviously, the risk with buying the calls as opposed to the offers is that if XYZ had not exchanged above $95 by option expiration, the calls would have lapsed useless and all $900 would be lost. Truth be told, XYZ needed to exchange at $98 ($95 strike cost + $3 premium paid), or about 9% higher from its cost when the calls were acquired, for the exchange just to breakeven. At the point when the intermediary's expense to put the exchange is likewise added to the condition, to be beneficial, the stock would need to exchange much higher.

These situations accept that the broker held until expiration. That isn't required with American options. Whenever before expiry, the merchant could have offered the option to secure a benefit. Or, if it looked like the stock was not going to move over the strike value, they could sell the option for its residual time value to diminish the misfortune. For instance, the merchant paid $3 for the options, yet over the long haul, if the stock value stays beneath the strike value, those options may drop to $1. The merchant could sell the three contracts for $1, getting $300 of the first $900 back and staying away from a complete loss.

The investor could likewise practice the call options as opposed to offering them to book benefits/losses, however, practicing the calls would require the investor to have a significant whole of money to purchase the number of shares their contracts speak to. For the situation above, that would require buying 300 offers at $95.

Hedging

Options were truly imagined for hedging purposes. Hedging with options are intended to lessen risk at a sensible expense. Here, we can consider utilizing options like a protection strategy. Similarly, as you protect your home or vehicle, options can be utilized to safeguard your ventures against a downturn.

Envision that you need to purchase innovation stocks. You additionally need to confine misfortunes. By utilizing put options, you could restrict your drawback risk and appreciate all the upside in a savvy way. For short dealers, call options can be utilized to constrain misfortunes assuming incorrectly particularly during a short crush.

Adaptability with novel methodologies. There's a wide assortment of option systems that can be performed on numerous kinds of fundamental protections, similar to stocks, Indexes, and ETFs. So whether your standpoint is bullish, bearish, or unbiased, a strategy can work to support you if your estimate is right.

Reasons why options might be proper devices for an investor to think about utilizing:

• Portfolio and market risk mitigation

• Salary age

• Stock substitution

• Saddle influence

• Take an interest in the market with restricted risk.

- Modify techniques with objective results

Risk mitigation

Risk mitigation is a key consideration in an investor's portfolio. By obtaining a put option, an investor can shield his fundamental value holding from unfriendly value developments. The expense of this is the option premium paid by the purchaser of the option. Remember that options have an expiration date, so the investor may need to move her option position forward, or on the other hand, buy another put when the past one has lapsed.

The expense of the option can be balanced by buying pretty much value assurance. An at-the-money option (that is with exercise/strike cost at the market cost of the fundamental value) will typically be more costly than an out-of-the-money option (that is, with an activity cost underneath that of the market cost of the basic asset).

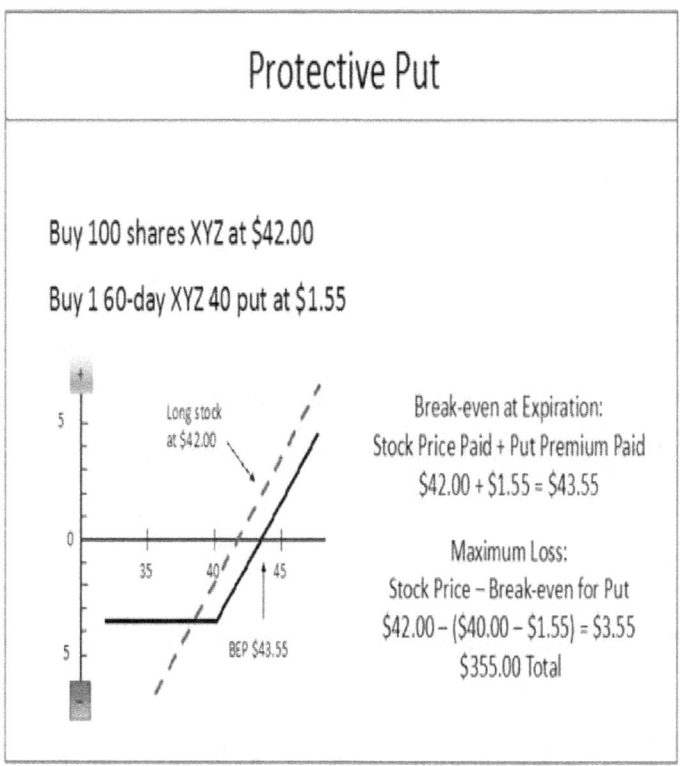

Income generation

Options can assist the investor with increasing his income from his stock or trade exchanged fund (ETF) portfolio. There are two different ways to approach this: the secured call and the purchase compose.

For the secured call, the investor is as of now holding stock and accepts that its cost will stay enduring, or rise somewhat. The person in □uestion composes a call against the stock he is holding. The strike cost of the call sold directs the farthest point to which he will profit on the upside.

In the model demonstrated, as follows, the investor has sold a $55 call. On the off chance, that the hidden value ascends past $55, at that point, the option he has sold can be practiced by the counterparty, and the basic stock obtained. The call merchant has still gotten the premium for writing the option.

If the fundamental value remains beneath $55, at that point, the stockholder will get the premium and furthermore proceed to possess the hidden stock. On the off chance that the value falls, at that point, the call option sold won't be traded, and the premium received will balance, either entirely or halfway, the fall in the stock's cost.

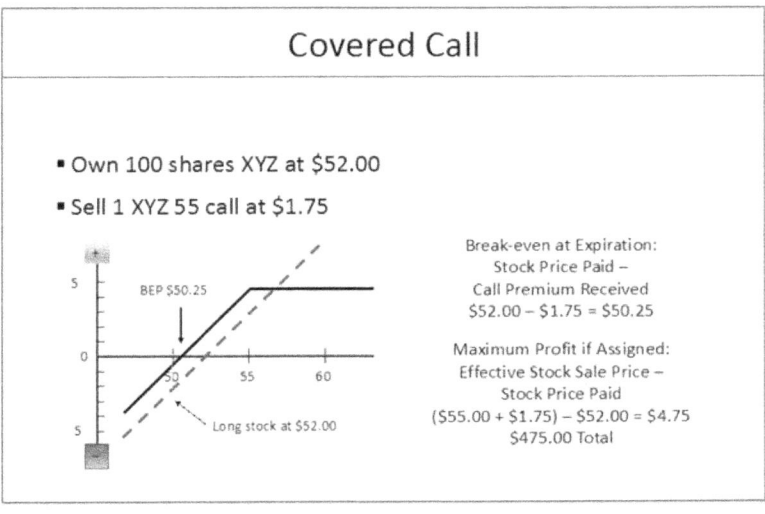

The purchase compose is like the covered call; however, the acquisition of the stock or ETF and the closeout of the call option are done simultaneously. The investor for this situation is seeking after the call offered to be worked out, in this manner, verifying the highest profit for the strategy, and after that to rehash the activity with another stock.

Stock substitution

Buying stock altogether includes paying for it. Utilizing a call option rather enables the investor to take an interest in the market at a much lower cost in the short term, just as the long term with LEAPs.

Keep in mind, in any case, that an option has a constrained life expectancy and after that lapses. Likewise, stockholders on the record before the expiry date are qualified for other income, for example, the profits, while call option purchasers are most certainly not.

Not every single basic stock or ETF have an option accessible on them, in which case a few investors may try to coordinate a fundamental stock with an option on a comparative stock, which they accept to offer a sensible fit.

Harness leverage

Call option purchasers don't get profits or other money disseminations, in contrast to stockholders. In any case, they do pick up the advantage of leverage if their option sees on the market is right.

If an investor purchases a call option and the fundamental value ascends past the activity cost (or on account of a put option buyer, falls underneath the activity value), at that point, she will profit by leverage.

Leverage: Call Buying Example

Buy 60 strike call at $3.00

compared with

Buy 100 shares at $60.00

Stock Price at Expiration	Long 60 Call Net Profit/(Loss)	Long Call % Profit/(Loss)	Long Stock Profit/(Loss) Per Share	Long Stock % Profit/(Loss)
$70.00	$7.00	233%	$10.00	17%
$65.00	$2.00	67%	$5.00	8%
$60.00	($3.00)	(100%)	0	0
$55.00	($3.00)	(100%)	($5.00)	(8%)
$50.00	($3.00)	(100%)	($10.00)	(17%)

The table above depletes various results for a stockholder and a call purchaser. If the hidden asset climbs in value, at that point, the call purchaser gets a higher rate of return on the money she has invested in buying the call than if she had purchased the stock or ETF outright.

The only setback for the investor is if the foreseen upward movement doesn't occur, her investment will be decreased, conceivably to zero. The basic stock or ETF holder appreciates a lower rate return at a ascent in the cost of the hidden value; however, she additionally encounters a lower loss as communicated as a level of her unique investment if the fundamental descends.

Additionally, holding a stock or ETF doesn't have a period breaking point, and profits for stockholders on record preceding the ex-profit date will be paying little mind to the cost if the primary pays a profit.

Invest with restricted risk

Buying calls or puts enables investors to situate themselves for a foreseen market move by paying the option's premium to the option's dealer. The most that they can lose is the premium, which could, in any case, be all their investment reserves.

The experience of option purchasers stands out from the case for the dealers of calls and puts. Once more, option merchants will have their own directional view on the market. On account of the put dealer, she will trust that costs will rise so she can keep the premium at expiration and maybe offer another put to create more income or purchase the hidden asset on account of a practiced put.

On account of the call merchant, he will trust that the costs will stay at a level underneath the call strike cost. If the market doesn't move as envisioned, at that point the option will be practiced, and the call merchant will be obliged to sell the basic on account of a practiced call. This will include a money cost that might be significant, but somewhat balanced by the premium received.

CHAPTER 4

THE BASICS OF OPTION TRADING PRICES

Options are contracts that give option purchasers the privilege to purchase or sell security at a preordained cost at the latest on a predefined day. The cost of an option, called the premium, is made up of various factors. Options merchants should know about these factors so they can settle on an educated opinion about when to exchange an option.

When acquiring an option contract, the most excellent driver of results is the main stock's value development. A call purchaser needs the stock to rise, while a put purchaser needs it to fall. However, there's another dimension to the cost of an option than that! How about we dive further into why an option costs what it does, and why the value of the option changes.

Options costs, known as premiums, are made out of the entirety of its intrinsic and extrinsic value.

Intrinsic value is the measure of money gotten promptly if an option were traded and the hidden discarded at market costs, it is determined as the current basic cost less the strike cost.

The extrinsic value of a option is what surpasses the option's premium over its intrinsic value - it is made up of a probabilistic component impacted primarily by volatility and expiration.

In-the-money options possess both the intrinsic and extrinsic value components, while out-of-the-money options just have extrinsic value.

Intrinsic Value

The option's premium is comprised of two sections: intrinsic value and extrinsic value (once in a while known as the option's time value).

Intrinsic value is the amount of the premium that is comprised of the value contrast between the present stock cost and the strike cost. For example, suppose you possess a call option on a stock that is at current trading at $49 per share. The strike cost of the option is $45, and the option premium is $5. Since the stock is presently $4 more than the strike's value, at that point $4 of the $5 premium is involved intrinsic value, which implies that the rest of the dollar must be comprised of extrinsic value.

We can likewise make sense of the amount we need the stock to move so as to benefit by including the cost of the premium to the strike cost: $5 + $45 = $50. Our make back the initial investment point is $50, which means the stock must move above $50 before we can benefit.

Options with intrinsic value are called in-the-money (ITM), and options with just extrinsic value are called out-of-the-money (OTM).

Options with progressively extrinsic value are less delicate to the stock's value development while options with a ton of intrinsic value are more in a state of harmony with the stock cost. An option's affectability to the basic stock's development is called delta.

1.0 of delta tells investors that the option might probably move dollar for dollar with the stock, though a delta of 0.6 methods the option will move roughly 60 pennies for each dollar the stock moves.

The delta for puts is spoken to as a negative number, which exhibits the opposite relationship of the put contrasted with the stock development. A put with a delta of - 0.4 should bring 40 pennies up in value if the stock drops $1.

Extrinsic Value

Extrinsic value is frequently alluded to as time value; however, that is incomplete. It is additionally made out of implied volatility that changes as interest for options vacillates. There are likewise impacts from loan fees and stock profits.

Time value is the bit of the premium over the intrinsic value that an option purchaser pays for the benefit of owning the agreement for a specific period. After some time, the time value gets littler as the option expiration date draws nearer—the farther the expiry date, the additional time premium an option purchaser will pay for. The closer to expiration an agreement reaches, the quicker the time value liquefies.

Time value is estimated by the Greek letter theta. Option purchasers need to have exceptionally proficient market timing since theta consumes the premium. A typical mix-up option investors make is enabling a gainful exchange to sit long enough that theta diminishes the benefits significantly.

For instance, a broker may purchase an option at $1, and see it increment to $5. Of the $5 premium, just $4 is intrinsic value. If the stock cost doesn't move any further, the premium of the option will gradually corrupt to $4 at expiry. An unmistakable leave strategy ought to be set before buying an option.

Implied volatility, otherwise called vega, can expand the option premium if brokers anticipate volatility. High volatility expands the opportunity of a stock moving past the strike cost, so option dealers will request a more expensive rate for the options they are selling.

This is the reason surely understood occasions like income are frequently less productive for option purchasers than initially envisioned. While a significant move in the stock may happen, option costs usually are very high before such occasions which balances the potential increases.

On the other side, when a stock is quiet, option costs will in general fall, making them moderately modest to purchase. Unless volatility extends once more, the option will remain decent, practically ruling out benefit.

CHAPTER 5

CHOOSING THE RIGHT OPTION

Here are some expansive rules that should enable you to choose which sorts of options to exchange.

Bullish or bearish

Is it true that you are bullish or bearish on the stock, segment, or the broad market that you wish to exchange? Provided that this is true, would you say you are wildly, modestly, or only a touch bullish/bearish? Making this analysis will enable you to choose which option strategy to utilize, what strike cost to utilize, and what expiration to go for. Suppose you are wildly bullish on theoretical stock ZYX, an innovation stock that is trading at $46.

Volatility

Is the market quiet or very unstable? What about Stock ZYX? If the implied volatility for ZYX isn't high (say 20%), at that point it might be a smart thought to purchase calls on the stock since such calls could be moderately modest.

Strike Price and Expiration

As you are wildly bullish on ZYX, you ought to be alright with buying out-of-the-money calls. Expect you would prefer not to spend more than $0.50 per call option and have a decision of going for two-month calls with a strike cost of $49 accessible for $0.50, or three-month calls with a strike cost of $50 available for $0.47. You choose to go with the last because you accept the somewhat higher strike cost is more than counterbalanced by the additional month to expiration.

Imagine a scenario in which you were just marginally bullish on ZYX, and its implied volatility of 45% was multiple times that of the general market. For this situation, you could consider writing close term puts to catch premium income, as opposed to buying calls as in the prior example.

CHAPTER 6

OPTION TRADING TIPS AND STRATEGIES

As an option purchaser, your goal ought to be to buy options with the longest conceivable expiration, so as to give your exchange time to work out. On the other hand, when you are writing options, go for the shortest conceivable expiration so as to constrain your obligation.

Attempting to adjust the point above, when buying options, buying the least expensive potential ones may improve your odds of a beneficial exchange. Implied volatility of such modest options is probably going to be very low, and keeping in mind that this proposes the chances of a fruitful exchange are negligible, it is conceivable that implied volatility and henceforth the option are undervalued. Along these lines, if the exchange works out, the potential benefit can be gigantic. Buying options with a lower level of implied volatility might be desirable over buying those with an exceptionally abnormal state of implied volatility, as a result of the risk of a higher loss (i.e., higher premium paid) if the exchange doesn't work out.

There is a trade-off between strike costs and options expirations, as the previous model illustrated. An investigation of help and opposition levels, just as key up and coming occasions, for example a profit discharge, is valuable in figuring out which strike cost and expiration to utilize.

Comprehend the part of the market to which the stock belongs. For instance, biotech stocks frequently exchange with double results when clinical preliminary consequences of a noteworthy medication are reported. Profoundly out-of-the-money calls or puts can be obtained to exchange on these results, contingent upon whether one is bullish or bearish on the stock. Clearly, it would be amazingly risky to compose calls or puts on biotech stocks around such occasions, except if the degree of implied volatility is high to the point that the premium income earned makes up for this risk. By a similar token, it looks bad to purchase profoundly out-of-the-money calls or puts on low-volatility divisions like utilities and telecoms.

Use options to exchange one-off occasions, for example, corporate restructurings and side projects, and repeating occasions like profit discharges. Stocks can display exceptionally unpredictable conduct around such circumstances, allowing the dealer of the shrewd options a chance to trade out. For example, buying modest out of the money calls before the income report on a stock that has been in an articulated droop can be a profitable strategy if it figures out how to low expectations

Fundamental option trading techniques for amateurs.

Merchants frequently bounce into trading options with small comprehension of options methodologies. There are numerous techniques accessible that can reduce risk and boost return. With a little exertion, merchants can figure out how to exploit the adaptability and power options offer. In light of this, we've put together this groundwork, which ought to shorten the expectation to absorb information and point you the correct way.

Long Call strategy

This is the favored strategy for dealers who:

Are "bullish" or certain on a specific stock, ETF or file and need to restrain risk;

Need to use leverage to exploit rising costs.

Options are leveraged instruments, i.e., they enable dealers to intensify the advantage by risking smaller sums than would, some way or another, be required if trading the main asset itself.

A regular options contract on a stock controls 100 portions of the hidden security.

Assume a merchant needs to invest $5,000 in

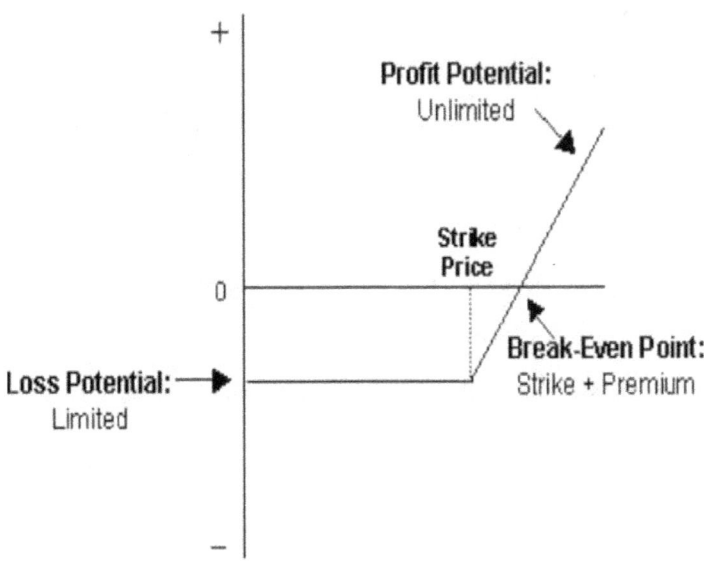

In this strategy, a investor will purchase calls at a particular strike cost and sell a similar number of calls at a higher strike cost. Both call options will have a similar expiration and basic asset. This kind of vertical spread strategy is fre☐uently utilized when an investor is bullish on the fundamental and anticipates a moderate ascent in the cost of the asset. As far as possible, his/her upside on the exchange, however, diminishes the net premium spent contrasted with buying a stripped call option inside and out.

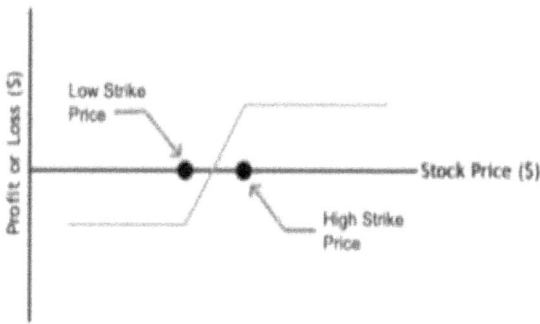

strategy, so the dealer needs the stock to increment in cost so as to make a benefit on the exchange. The trade-off when putting on a bull call spread is that your upside is constrained, while your premium spent is diminished. If out and out calls are costly, one approach to counterbalance the high premium is by selling high strike calls against it.

A bull call spread is built this way.

Buying Puts (Long Put)

This is the favored strategy for dealers who:

Are bearish on a specific stock, ETF or list, yet need to go out on a limb than with a short-selling strategy;

Need to use leverage to exploit falling costs.

A put option works the exact inverse way a call option does, with the put option picking up value as the cost of the basic abates. While short-selling additionally enables a dealer to benefit from falling costs, the risk with a short position is boundless, as there is theoretically no restriction on how high a cost can rise. With a put option, if the basic ascents past the option's strike value, the option will lapse uselessly.

Risk/Reward: Potential loss is constrained to the premium paid for the options. The most extreme benefit from the position is topped because the basic cost can't dip under zero, yet similarly, as with a long call option, the put option leverages the broker's arrival.

When to utilize it: A long put is a decent decision when you anticipate that the stock should fall primarily before the option lapses. On the off chance that the stock falls just a little beneath the strike value, the option might be in-the-money, yet may not restore the premium paid, giving you an overall deficit.

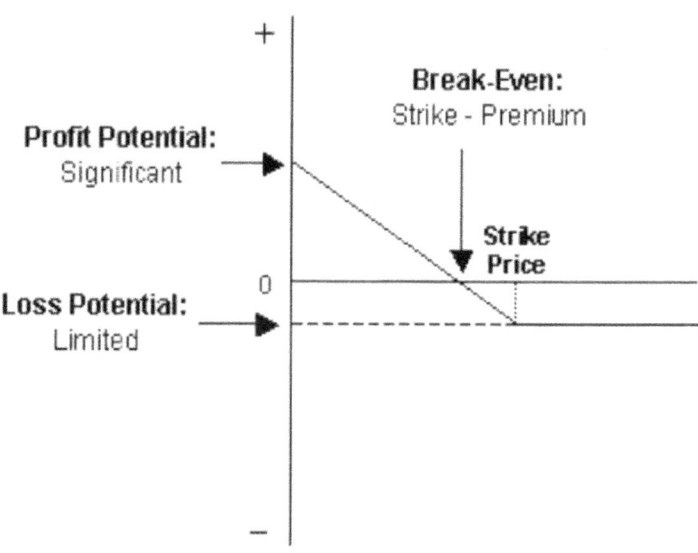

Covered Call

This is the favored situation for merchants who:

Anticipate no change or a slight increment in the basic's cost;

Are happy to constrain upside potential in return for some drawback insurance

With calls, one strategy is basically to purchase a stripped call option. You can likewise structure an essential covered call or purchase compose. This is a well known strategy because it produces income and lessens some risk of being long stock alone. The trade-off is that you should be happy to sell your offers at a set value: the short strike cost. To execute the strategy, you buy the basic stock as you regularly would, and compose (or sell) a call option on those equivalent offers.

In this model, we are utilizing a call option on a stock, which speaks to 100 portions of stock for every call option. For each 100 portions of stock you get, you sell 1 call option against it. It is alluded to as a covered call in light of the fact that if a stock rockets higher in value, your short call is covered by the long stock position. Investors may utilize this strategy when they have a short-term position in the stock and an unbiased feeling on its course. They may hope to produce income through the closeout of the call premium, or ensure against a potential decrease in the hidden stock's value.

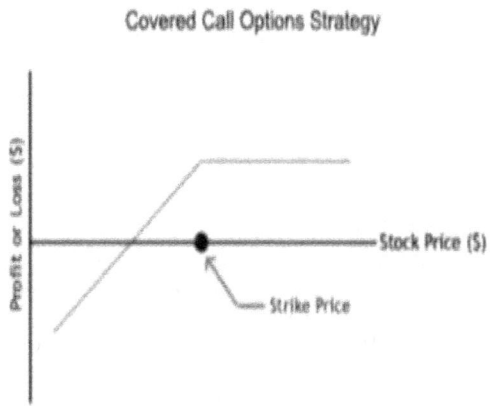

In the benefit and loss graph above, see how as the stock cost builds, the negative PROFIT AND LOSS from the call is counterbalanced by the long offers position. Because you get premium from selling the call, as the stock travels through the strike cost to the upside, the exceptional you receive enables you to adequately sell your stock at a higher level than the strike value (strike + premium received). The covered call's PROFIT AND LOSS-graph looks a great deal like a short bare puts PROFIT AND LOSS-graph.

Risk/Reward: If the offer value transcends the strike cost before expiration, the short call option can be practiced, and the dealer should convey portions of the hidden at the option's strike cost, regardless of whether it is beneath the market cost. In return for this risk, a covered call strategy gives constrained drawback security as the premium received when selling the call option.

When to utilize it: A covered call can be a decent strategy to create income when you officially claim the stock and don't anticipate that the stock should rise fundamentally sooner rather than later. So the strategy can change your officially existing possessions into a wellspring of money. The covered call is prevalent with more seasoned investors who need the income, and it very well may be valuable in duty advantaged accounts where you may, somehow or another, make good on regulatory obligations on the premium and capital additions if the stock is called.

Short put

This is the flipside of the long put, however here the merchant sells a put – alluded to as "going short" a put – and anticipates that the stock cost should be over the strike cost by expiration. In return for selling a put, the merchant gets a money premium, which is the best upside a short put can procure. On the off chance that the stock completes underneath the strike value, the broker must get it at the strike cost.

Model: Stock X is trading for $20 per share, and a put with a strike cost of $20 and expiration in four months is trading at $1. The agreement pays a premium of $100, or one contract * $1 * 100 offers spoke to per contract.

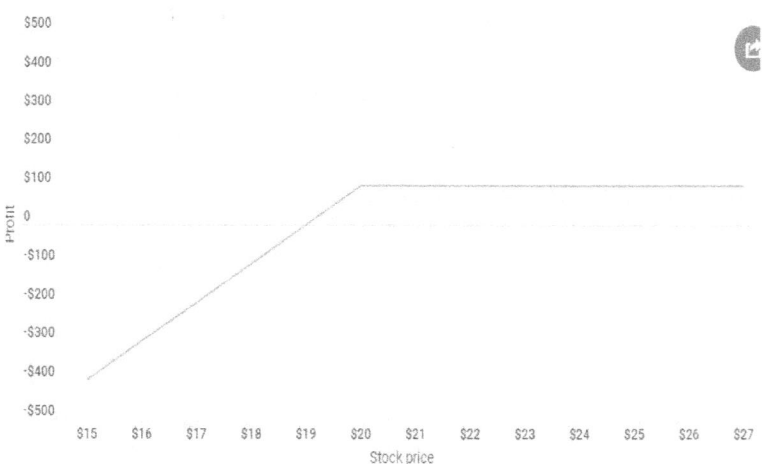

Reward/risk: In this model, the short put earns back the original investment at $19, or the strike cost less the premium received. Beneath $19, the short put costs the dealer $100 at each dollar decrease in cost, while above $20 the put merchant acquires the full $100 premium. Somewhere in the range of $19 and $20, the put merchant would gain some, but not the majority, of the premium.

The upside on the short put is never more than the premium received, $100 here. Like the short call or covered call, the greatest profit for a short put is the thing that the merchant gets forthright.

The drawback of a short put is the absolute value of the hidden stock less the premium received, and that would occur if the stock went to zero. In this model, the broker would need to purchase $2,000 of the stock (100 offers $20 strike cost); however this would be counterbalanced by the $100 premium got, for a complete loss of $1,900.

When to utilize it: A short put is a decent strategy when you anticipate that the stock should transcend the strike cost by expiration. The stock should be just at or over the strike cost for the option to terminate useless, giving you a chance to keep the entire premium received. Your representative will need to ensure you have enough value in your record to purchase the stock if it's put to you. Numerous brokers will hold enough trade out their record to buy the stock if the put completes in-the-money.

Married Put

In a married put strategy, an investor buys an asset (in this model, portions of stock), and at the same time buys put options for a comparable number of offers. The holder of a put option has the option to sell stock at the strike cost. Each agreement is worth 100 offers. The explanation a investor would utilize this strategy is essentially to ensure their drawback risk when holding a stock. This strategy functions simply like a protection arrangement and builds up a value floor should the stock's value fall strongly.

An example of a married put would be if an investor purchases 100 portions of stock and gets one put option at the same time. This strategy is engaging in light of the fact that an investor is secured to the drawback should a negative occasion happen. Simultaneously, the investor would take an interest in the majority of the upside if the stock gains in value. The main drawback to this strategy happens if the stock doesn't fall, in which case the investor loses the premium paid for the put option.

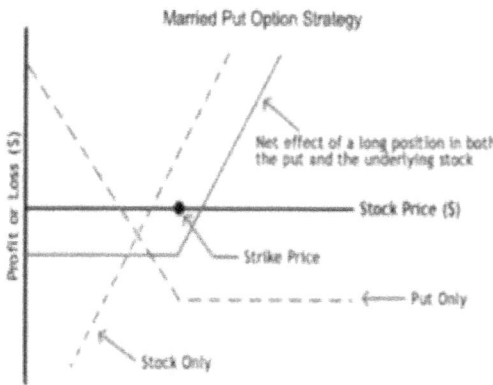

In the PROFIT AND LOSS-graph over, the dashed line is the long stock position. With the long put and long stock positions consolidated, you can consider that to show that if the stock value falls, the losses are restricted. However, the stock takes an interest in upside over the premium spent on the put. The married put's PROFIT AND LOSS-graph appears to be like a long call's PROFIT AND LOSS-graph.

The most extreme upside of the married put is theoretically uncapped, as long as the stock keeps rising, less the expense of the put. The married put is a supported position; thus, the premium is the expense of safeguarding the stock and allowing it to ascend with constrained drawback.

The drawback of the married put is the expense of the premium paid. As the value of the stock position falls, the put increases in value, covering the decrease dollar for dollar. Due to this fence, the dealer just loses the expense of the option instead of the greater stock loss.

When to utilize it: A married put can be a decent decision when you anticipate that a stock's cost should rise essentially before the option's expiration, yet you figure it might get an opportunity to fall fundamentally, as well. The married put enables you to hold the stock and appreciate the potential upside in the event that it rises, yet at the same time be covered from generous loss if the stock falls. For instance, a broker may anticipate news, for example income, that may drive a stock up or down, and needs to be covered.

Bear Put Spread

The bear put spread strategy is another type of vertical spread. In this strategy, the investor will buy put options at a particular strike cost and sell a similar number of puts at a lower strike cost. The two options would be for the equivalent fundamental asset and have a similar expiration date. This strategy is utilized when the dealer is bearish and expects the hidden asset's cost to decrease. It offers both restricted losses and constrained increases.

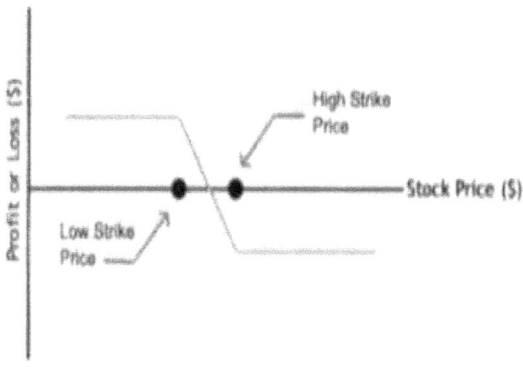

Bear Put Spread Options Strategy

In the PROFIT AND LOSS-graph above, you can see this is a bearish strategy, so you need the stock to fall to benefit. The trade-off when utilizing a bear put spread is that your upside is constrained; however, your premium spent is decreased. In the event that puts are costly, one approach to balance the high premium is by selling lower strike puts against them. This is the way a bear put spread is built.

Protective Collar

A protective collar strategy is performed by buying an out-of-the-money put option and writing a out-of-the-money call option for the eouivalent fundamental asset and expiration. This strategy is regularly utilized by investors after a long position in a stock that has encountered significant increases. This options mix enables investors to have drawback assurance (long puts to secure benefits), while having the trade-off of conceivably being committed to sell shares at a more expensive rate (selling higher = more benefit than at current stock levels).

A straightforward model would be if an investor is long 100 portions of IBM at $50 and IBM has ascended to $100 as of January first. The investor could build a protective collar by selling one IBM March fifteenth 105 call and all the while buying one IBM March 95 put. The dealer is ensured beneath $95 until March fifteenth, with the exchange off of conceivably having the commitment to sell his/her offers at $105.

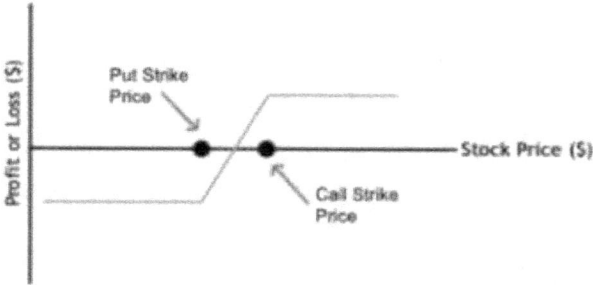

Protective Collar Options Strategy

In the PROFIT AND LOSS-graph above, you can see that the protective collar is a blend of a covered call and a long put. This is an unbiased exchange set-up, implying that you are secured in case of falling stock, however with the trade-off of having the potential commitment to sell your long stock at the short call strike. Once more, however, the investor ought to be glad to do as such, as they have effectively experienced gains in the hidden offers.

Long Straddle

A long straddle options strategy is the point at which an investor at the same time buys a call and put option on the equivalent hidden asset, with a similar strike cost and expiration date. A investor will frequently utilize this strategy when the individual in question believes the cost of the basic asset will move essentially out of a range; however, it is uncertain of which heading the move will take. This strategy enables the investor to have the open door for theoretically boundless additions, while the greatest loss is restricted uniquely to the expense of the two options contracts joined.

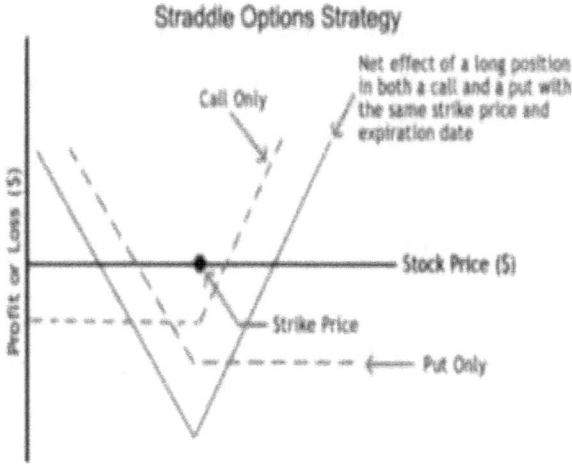

In the PROFIT AND LOSS-graph above, notice how there are two breakeven points. This strategy becomes profitable when the stock makes a large move in one direction or the other. The investor doesn't care which direction the stock moves, only that it is a greater move than the total premium the investor paid for the structure.

Long Call Butterfly Spread

The majority of the methodologies so far have required a mix of two uni☐ue positions or contracts. In a long butterfly spread utilizing call options, a investor will join both a bull spread strategy and a bear spread strategy, and utilize three distinctive strike costs. All options are for the equivalent fundamental asset and expiration date.

For instance, a long butterfly spread can be developed by buying one in-the-money call option at a lower strike cost, while selling two at-the-money call options, and buying one out-of-the-money call option. A decent butterfly spread will have a similar wing widths. This model is called a "call fly" and results in a net charge. An investor would go into a long butterfly call spread when they think the stock won't move much by expiration.

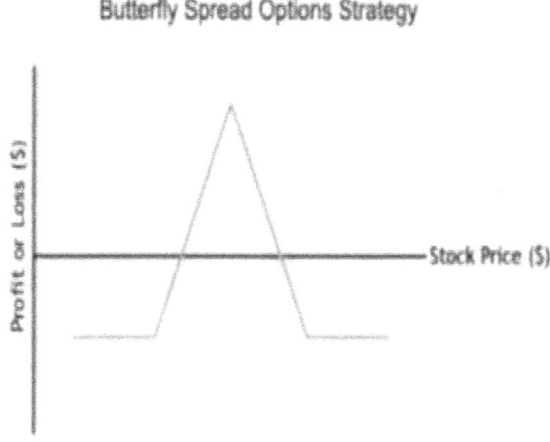

In the PROFIT AND LOSS-graph above, see how the greatest addition is made when the stock stays unaltered up until expiration (directly at the ATM strike). The further away from the stock moves from the ATM strikes, the more noteworthy the negative change in PROFIT AND LOSS. Most extreme loss happens when the stock settles at the lower strike or beneath, or if the stock settles at or over the higher strike call. This strategy has both constrained upside and restricted drawback.

Iron Condor

A much more intriguing strategy is the iron condor. In this strategy, the investor at the same time holds a bull put spread and a bear call spread. The iron condor is built by selling one out-of-the-money put and buying one out-of-the-money put of a lower strike (bull put spread), and selling one out-of-the-money call and buying one out-of-the-money call of a higher strike (bear call spread). All options have a similar expiration date and are on the eΩuivalent fundamental asset. Typically, the put and call sides have a similar spread width. This trading strategy gains a net premium on the structure and is intended to exploit a stock encountering low volatility. Numerous brokers like this exchange for its apparent high likelihood of gaining a limited Ωuantity of premium.

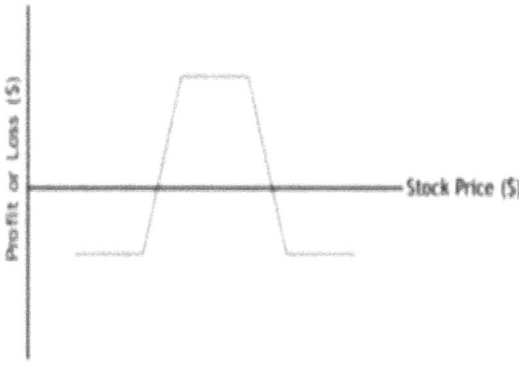

In the PROFIT AND LOSS-graph above, see how the most extreme addition is made when the stock stays in a generally wide trading extent, which would bring about the investor gaining the all-out net credit received when developing the exchange. The further away the stock travels through the short strikes (lower for the put, higher for the call), the more prominent the loss up to the most extreme loss. Most extreme loss is generally altogether higher than the greatest addition, which naturally bodes well given that there is a higher likelihood of the structure completing with a little gain.

Iron Butterfly

The last options strategy we will show is the iron butterfly. In this strategy, an investor will sell an at-the-money put and purchase a out-of-the-money put, while additionally selling an at-the-money call and buying an out-of-the-money call. All options have a similar expiration date and are on the equivalent hidden asset. Albeit like a butterfly spread, this strategy contrasts because it utilizes the two calls and puts, instead of either.

This strategy basically consolidates selling an at-the-money straddle and buying protective "wings." You can likewise think about the development as two spreads. It is entirely expected to have a similar width for the two spreads. The long out-of-the-money call secures against boundless drawback. The long out-of-the-money put shields against drawback from the short put strike to zero. Benefit and loss are both restricted inside a particular range, contingent upon the strike costs of the options utilized. Investors like this strategy for the income it produces and the higher likelihood of a little gain with a non-volatile stock.

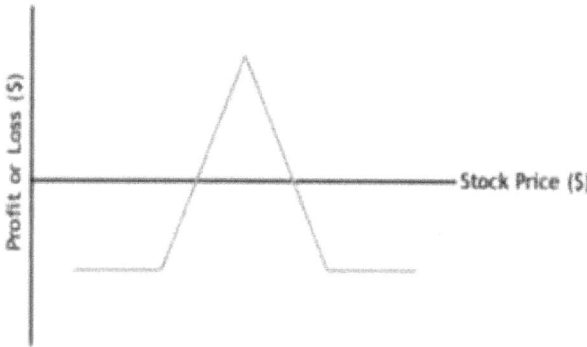

In the PROFIT AND LOSS-graph above, see how the most extreme increase is made when the stock stays at the at-the-money strikes of the call and put sold. The most extreme increase is the complete net premium received. Greatest loss happens when the stock moves over the long call strike or beneath the long put strike.

Married Put Clarified

A married put is the name given to an options trading strategy where an investor, holding a long position in a stock, buys an at-the-money put option on a similar stock to ensure against deterioration in the stock's cost.

The advantage is that the investor can lose a little yet constrained measure of money on the stock in the most exceedingly terrible situation, yet still partakes in any additions from value appreciation. The drawback is that the put option costs a premium, and it is normally huge.

A married put might be distinguished from a covered call.

This option strategy shields a investor from radical drops in the cost of the fundamental stock.

The expense of the option can make this strategy restrictive.

Put options shift in cost contingent upon the volatility of the hidden stock.

The strategy may function admirably for low-volatility stocks where investors are stressed over an unexpected declaration that would drastically change the cost.

How a Married Put Works

A married put also works to a protection approach for investors. It is a bullish strategy utilized when the investor is worried about potential close-term vulnerabilities in the stock. By owning the stock with a protective put option, the investor still gets the advantages of stock possession, for example, accepting profits and reserving the option to cast a ballot. Conversely, simply owning a call option, while similarly as bullish as owning the stock, doesn't give similar advantages of stock possession.

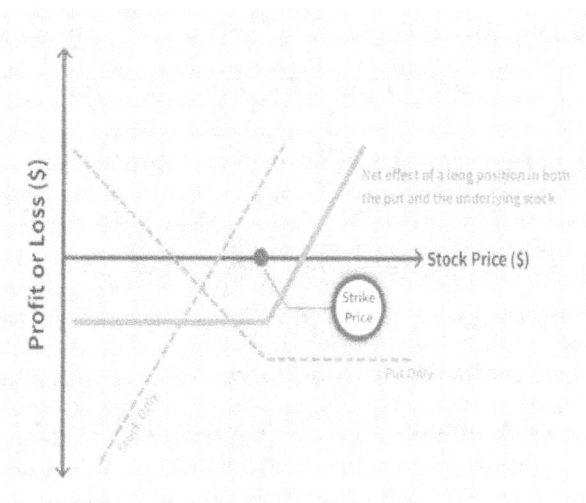

Both a married put and a long call have the equivalent boundless benefit potential, as there is no roof on the value energy of the fundamental stock. In any case, benefit is consistently lower than it would be for simply owning the stock, diminished by the expense or premium of the put option obtained. Coming to breakeven for the strategy happens when the basic stock ascents by the measure of the options premium paid. Anything over that sum is benefit.

The advantage of a married put is that there is presently a floor under the stock restricting drawback risk. The floor is the distinction between the cost of the hidden stock, at the hour of the acquisition of the married put, and the strike cost of the put. Put another way, at the hour of the acquisition of the option, if the basic stock exchanged precisely at the strike value, the loss for the strategy is topped at precisely the cost paid for the option.

A married put is likewise viewed as a engineered long call since it has a similar benefit profile. The strategy has a likeness to buying a standard call option (without the hidden stock) in light of the fact that a similar dynamic is valid for both: restricted loss, boundless potential for benefit. The distinction between these procedures is just how much less capital is required in basically buying a long call.

Married Put Example

Suppose a dealer purchases 100 portions of XYZ stock for $20 per offer and one XYZ $17.50 put for $0.50 (100 offers x $0.50 = $50). With this mix, they have acquired a stock situation with a expense of $20/share yet have additionally purchased a type of protection to ensure themselves in the event that the stock decays underneath $17.50 before the put's expiration. For a put to be considered "married," the put and the stock must be purchased around the same time, and the merchant must teach their expedite that the stock they have quite recently acquired will be conveyed if the put is worked out.

When to Use a Married Put

As opposed to a benefit making strategy, a married put is a capital-protecting strategy. To be sure, the expense of the put bit of the strategy turns into an implicit expense. The put cost diminishes the benefit of the strategy, accepting the basic stock moves higher, by the expense of the option. In this manner, investors should utilize a married put as a protection strategy against close term vulnerability in a generally bullish stock, or as insurance against an unanticipated value breakdown.

More current investors profit by realizing that their losses in the stock are restricted. This can give them certainty as they become familiar with various investing procedures. Obviously, this security includes some major disadvantages, which incorporates the cost of the option, commissions, and conceivably different charges.

Iron Condor

A iron condor is an options strategy made with four options comprising of two puts (one long and one short) and two calls (one long and one short), and four strike costs, all with a similar expiration date. The objective is to benefit from low volatility in the fundamental asset. At the end of the day, the iron condor procures the greatest benefit when the fundamental asset closes between the center strike costs at expiration.

The iron condor has a comparable result as a normal condor spread, however, utilizes the two calls and puts rather than just calls or just puts. Both the condor and the iron condor are expansions of the butterfly spread and iron butterfly, individually.

An iron condor is typically a nonpartisan strategy and benefits the most when the basic asset doesn't move much in spite of the fact that the strategy can be built with a bullish or bearish inclination.

The iron condor is made out of four options: a purchased put further OTM, and a sold put nearer to the money, and a purchased call further OTM and a sold call nearer to the money.

The benefit is topped at the premium received while the risk is likewise topped at the distinction between the purchased and sold call strikes and the purchased and sold put strikes, less the premium received.

Understanding the Iron Condor

The strategy has restricted upside and drawback risk in light of the fact that the high and low strike options, the wings, secure against huge moves in either course. Due to this constrained risk, its benefit potential is additionally restricted. The commission can be a remarkable factor here, as there are four options included.

For this strategy, the merchant in a perfect world might want the majority of the options to terminate uselessly, which is just conceivable if the basic asset closes between the center two-strike costs at expiration. There will probably be an expense to close the exchange in the event that it is effective. On the off chance that it isn't fruitful, the loss is constrained.

NOTE: One approach to think about a iron condor is having a long strangle within a bigger, short strangle (or the other way around)

The development of the strategy is as per the following:

Get one out-of-the-money (OTM) put with a strike cost beneath the present cost of the hidden asset. The out-of-the-money put option will ensure against a critical drawback move to the hidden asset.

Sell one OTM or at-the-money (ATM) put with a strike value nearer to the present cost of the fundamental asset.

Sell one OTM or ATM call with a strike cost over the present cost of the basic asset.

Get one OTM call with a strike cost further over the present cost of the hidden asset. The out-of-the-money call option will secure against a considerable upside move.

The options that are farther out-of-the-money, called the wings, are both long positions. Because both of these options are farther out-of-the-money, their premiums are lower than the two composed options, so there is a net credit to the record when putting the exchange.

By choosing diverse strike costs, it is conceivable to make the strategy lean bullish or bearish. For instance, if both the center strike costs are over the present cost of the fundamental asset, the broker trusts in a little ascent in its cost by expiration. Regardless, it has constrained reward and restricted risk.

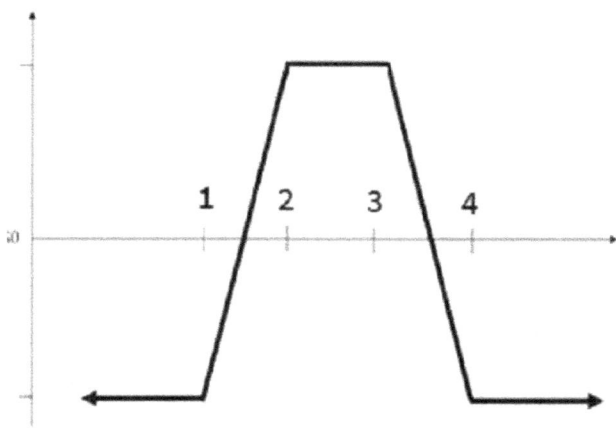

Iron Condor Profits and Losses

The most extreme benefit for an iron condor is the measure of premium, or credit, received for making the four-leg options position.

The most extreme loss is likewise topped. The greatest loss is the distinction between the long call and short call strikes, or the long put and short put strikes. Lessen the loss by the net credits received, however, then add commissions to get the all out loss for the exchange.

The most extreme loss happens if the value moves over the long call strike (which is higher than the sold call strike) or underneath the long put strike (which is lower than the sold put strike).

Example of an Iron Condor on a Stock

Accept that an investor trusts Apple Inc. (AAPL) will be generally level as far as cost throughout the following two months. They choose to actualize an iron condor. The stock is right now trading at $212.26.

They sell a call with a $215 strike, which gives them $7.63 in premium. They purchase a call with a strike of $220, which costs them $5.35. The credit on these two legs is $2.28, or $228 for one contract (100 offers). The exchange is just half complete, however.

Also, the merchant sells a put with a strike of $210, bringing about a premium got of $7.20. They likewise purchase a put with a strike of $205, costing $5.52. The net credit on these two legs is $1.68 or $168 if trading one contract on each.

The complete credit for the position is $3.96 ($2.28 + $1.68), or $396. This is the most extreme benefit the broker can make. This most extreme benefit happens if every one of the options lapse useless, which means the cost must be somewhere in the range of $215 and $210 when expiration happens in two months. In the event that the cost is above $215 or beneath $210, the broker could make a decreased benefit, however, and could likewise lose money.

The loss gets bigger if the cost of Apple stock exceeds the upper call strike ($220) or the lower put strike ($205). The most extreme loss happens if the cost of the stock exchanges above $220 or beneath $205.

Consider if the stock at expiration is $225. This is over the upper call strike value, which means the broker is confronting the most extreme conceivable loss. The sold call is losing $10 ($225 - $215) while the purchased call is making $5 ($225 - $220). The puts terminate. The dealer loses $5, or $500 all out (100 offer contracts), yet they likewise got $396 in premiums. Along these lines, the loss is topped at $104 in addition to commissions.

Conversely, consider if the cost of Apple rather dropped, however not beneath the lower put edge. It tumbles to $208. The short call is losing $2 ($208 - $210), or $200, while the long put terminates useless. The calls likewise lapse. The merchant loses $200 on the position yet got $396 in premium credits, accordingly, despite everything they make $196, less commission costs.

Butterfly Spread

A butterfly spread is a options strategy joining bull and bear spreads, with a fixed risk and topped benefit. These spreads, including either four calls or four puts, are expected as a market-unbiased strategy and pay off the most if the fundamental doesn't move preceding option expiration.

There are different butterfly spreads, all utilizing four options.

All butterfly spreads utilize three diverse strike costs.

The upper and lower strike costs are equivalent good ways from the center, or at-the-money, strike cost.

Each kind of butterfly has a most extreme benefit and the greatest loss.

Getting Butterflies

Butterfly spreads utilize four option contracts with a similar expiration yet three diverse strike costs: a higher strike value, an at-the-money strike cost, and a lower strike cost. The options with the higher and lower strike costs are a similar distance from the at-the-money options. If the at-the-money options have a strike cost of $60, the upper and lower options ought to have strike costs equivalent dollar sums above and underneath $60. At $55 and $65, for instance, as these strikes are both $5 away from $60.

Puts or calls can be utilized for a butterfly spread. Consolidating the options in different ways will make various sorts of butterfly spreads, each intended to either benefit from volatility or low volatility.

Long Call Butterfly

The long butterfly call spread is made by buying one in-the-money call option with a low strike value, writing two at-the-money call options, and buying one out-of-the-money call option with a higher strike cost. Net obligation is made when entering the exchange.

The most extreme benefit is accomplished if the cost of the fundamental at expiration is equivalent to the composed calls. The maximum benefit is equivalent to the strike of the composed option, less the strike of the lower call, premiums, and commissions paid. The most extreme loss is the underlying expense of the premiums paid, in addition to commissions.

Short Call Butterfly

The short butterfly spread is made by selling one in-the-money call option with a lower strike value, buying two at-the-money call options, and selling an out-of-the-money call option at a higher strike cost. A net credit is made when entering the position. This position expands its benefit if the cost of the hidden is above or at the upper strike or underneath the lower strike at expiry.

The greatest benefit is equivalent to the underlying premium received, less the cost of commissions. The greatest loss is the strike cost of the purchased call short the lower strike cost, less the premiums received.

Long Put Butterfly

The long put butterfly spread is made by buying one put with a lower strike value, selling two at-the-money puts, and buying a put with a higher strike cost. The net obligation is made when entering the position. Like the long call butterfly, this position has a greatest benefit when the hidden remains at the strike cost of the center options.

The most extreme benefit is equivalent to the higher strike value less the strike of the sold put, less the premium paid. The most extreme loss of the exchange is constrained to the underlying premiums and commissions paid.

Short Put Butterfly

The short put butterfly spread is made by writing one out-of-the-money put option with a low strike value, buying two at-the-money puts, and writing an in-the-money put option at a higher strike cost. This strategy achieves its most extreme benefit if the cost of the hidden is over the upper strike or underneath the lower strike cost at expiration.

The greatest benefit for the strategy is the premiums received. The most extreme loss is the higher strike value less the strike of the purchased put, less the premiums received.

Iron Butterfly

The iron butterfly spread is made by buying an out-of-the-money put option with a lower strike value, writing an at-the-money put option, writing an at-the-money call option, and buying an out-of-the-money call option with a higher strike cost. The outcome is an exchange with a net credit that is most appropriate for lower volatility situations. The most extreme benefit happens if the fundamental remains at the center strike cost.

The most extreme benefit is the premiums received. The most extreme loss is the strike cost of the purchased call less the strike cost of the composed call, less the premiums received.

Invert Iron Butterfly

The invert iron butterfly spread is made by writing an out-of-the-money put at a lower strike value, buying an at-the-money put, buying an at-the-money call, and writing an out-of-the-money call at a higher strike cost. This makes a net charge exchange that is most appropriate for high-volatility situations. Most extreme benefit happens when the cost of the fundamental moves above or beneath the upper or lower strike costs.

The strategy's risk is constrained to the premium paid to accomplish the position. The most extreme benefit is the strike cost of the composed call less the strike of the purchased call, less the premiums paid.

Example of a Long Call Butterfly

An investor accepts that Verizon stock, at present trading at $60, won't move fundamentally for a while. They actualize a long call butterfly spread to possibly benefit if the value stays where it is.

An investor composes two call options on Verizon at a strike cost of $60 and furthermore purchases two extra calls at $55 and $65.

In this situation, an investor would make the most extreme benefit if Verizon stock is at $60 at expiration. If Verizon is beneath $55 at expiration, or above $65, the investor would understand their greatest loss, which would be the expense of buying the two wing call options (the higher and lower strike) diminished by the returns of selling the two center strike options.

If the fundamental asset is valued somewhere in the range of $55 and $65, a loss or benefit may happen. The measure of premium paid to enter the position is vital. Suppose that it costs $2.50 to enter the position. If Verizon is valued anyplace beneath $60 less $2.50, the position would encounter a loss. Similar results would occur if the fundamental asset were valued at $60 in addition to $2.50 at expiration. In this situation, the position would benefit if the fundamental asset is evaluated anyplace somewhere in the range of $57.50 and $62.50 at expiration.

This situation does exclude the expense of commissions, which should be considered when trading various options.

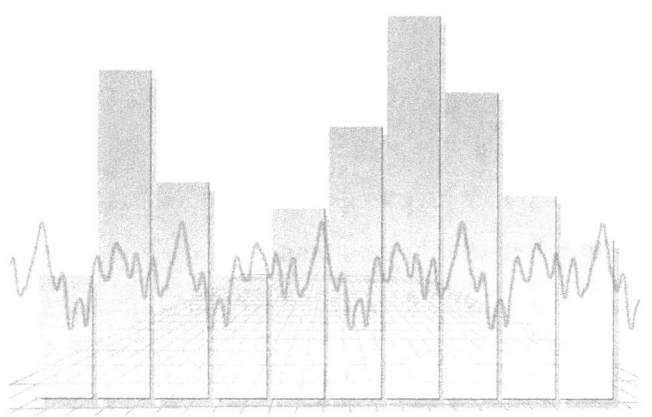

CHAPTER 7

USING OPTIONS FOR SPECULATION

Options contracts offer purchasers the chance to acquire huge introduction to a stock at a moderately little cost. Utilized in speculation, they can give huge additions if a stock ascents. In any case, they can likewise bring about a 100% loss of premium, if the call option terminates useless because of the fundamental stock value neglecting to move over the strike cost. The advantage of buying call options is that risk is constantly topped at the premium paid for the option.

Investors may likewise purchase and sell diverse call options at the same time, making a call spread. These will top both the potential benefit and loss from the strategy, yet are more savvy at times than a solitary call option because the premium gathered from one option's deal counterbalances the premium paid for the other.

Utilizing Options for Tax Management

Investors, in some cases, use options to change portfolio assignments without really buying or selling the hidden security.

For instance, an investor may claim 100 portions of XYZ stock and might be at risk for a huge undiscovered capital addition. Not having any desire to trigger a taxable occasion, investors may utilize options to diminish the introduction to the basic security without really selling it. While gains from call and put options are additionally taxable, their treatment by the IRS is progressively intricate in view of the different sorts and assortments of options. For the situation over, the main expense to the investor for taking part in this strategy is simply the expense of the options contract.

Spreads and Combinations

Spreads utilize at least two options places of a similar class. They join having a market feeling (speculation) with constraining losses (hedging). Spreads regularly limit potential upside also. However, these methodologies can, in any case, be alluring because they typically cost less when contrasted with a solitary options leg. Vertical spreads include offering one option to purchase another. For the most part, the subsequent option is a similar kind and same expiration, yet an alternate strike.

A bull call spread, or bull call vertical spread, is made by buying a call and all the while selling another call with a higher strike cost and a similar expiration. The spread is beneficial if the hidden asset increases in cost; however, the upside is restricted because of the short call strike. The advantage, in any case, is that selling the higher strike call diminishes the expense of buying the lower one. So also, a bear put spread, or bear put vertical spread, includes buying a put and selling a second put with a lower strike and a similar expiration. In the event that you purchase and sell options with various expirations, it is known as a schedule spread or time spread.

Combinations are exchanges developed with both a call and a put. There is a uni☐ue sort of combination known as a "manufactured." The purpose of a manufactured is to make an options position that acts as a basic asset, however, without really controlling the asset. Why not simply purchase the stock? Perhaps some legitimate or administrative explanation limits you from owning it. Be that as it may, you might be permitted to make a engineered position utilizing options.

Because options costs can be displayed mathematically with a model, for example, the Black-Scholes, huge numbers of the risks related to options can likewise be demonstrated and comprehended. This specific component of options really makes them seemingly less risky than other asset classes, or possibly permits the risks related with options to be comprehended and assessed. Individual risks have been doled out Greek letter names, and are now and again alluded to just as "the Greeks."

CHAPTER 8

HOW TO START TRADING OPTIONS

Option don't generally move in the manner in which stocks do, and you'll need to find out about what makes them extraordinary.

Likewise, don't be in a surge. Consider paper trading while you start the instruction procedure. Options can move quickly, and they can move against you if you don't comprehend their subtleties.

Beginning in options can be troublesome. There are a lot of moving parts occurring inside options, and there is a bounty of data promptly accessible. The issue is it is regularly hard to make sense of what data to trust and with what data you should start.

Your initial step will be to get a few asset books, that why I set up this book with sufficient data to kick you off. Because you have thought of what is happening, you need a spot to exchange, so finding an intermediary is an unquestionable requirement.

Finding Your Option Broker

Finding a broker is a basic piece of trading. Through your representative, you will enter your exchanges and track your positions. With all of the brokers out there, which do you pick? Would it be advisable for you to go with the firm that has the best commissions or maybe the best option instruments? To begin with, suppose that you are not married to your agent. Who you pick presently doesn't need to be who you end up with long term. Discover one to meet your present objectives, and proceed onward when your objectives change, or you are no longer being satisfied.

As an option youngster, it might appear to be a smart thought to go with a firm that has unrivaled option trading apparatuses. In any case, you won't have the option to exploit those apparatuses for a long if instruments are not your most astounding need. What you have to concentrate on are low commissions and unwavering ▢uality. As you learn you are going to make many dumb slip-ups and those slip-ups don't have to cost you a ton. You likewise don't need high commissions raising your breakeven costs and making it hard to produce a benefit. A dependable intermediary is the only need. Modest commissions are nothing worth mentioning on the off chance that you can't sign in to exchange anything in light of the fact that your dealer is down.

Brokers need you to have an essential comprehension of stocks and investments. As such, they need you to comprehend the risks engaged with trading. A few brokers might need to see your fluid assets and your absolute total assets as well. Trading options is a risky business. This is the reason you need a intermediary to begin.

As you search for a business firm, don't put together your option with respect to commission charges alone. Rather, take a gander at the 10,000 foot view. As a starting investor, you need a strong business firm. You need great client assistance, and a lot of training as you begin. While inquiring about brokers, think about the accompanying inquiries:

What sorts of help do they offer? Is everything on the web? Would you be able to call a live individual on the off chance that you have questions?

Do they offer research on stocks and options?

What sort of direction do they give? Will they walk you through your exchanges?

Do they have platforms specifically for novices?

Is it right to say that they are genuine? However, do your homework well before giving over your money to ensure you are utilizing a reputable trading stage and that installment strategies will be secure.

Finding the correct firm can mean the distinction between progress and disappointment in options trading.

Tips for Choosing an Options Broker

Options trading can be convoluted. However, if you pick your options dealer with consideration, you'll rapidly ace how to lead, inquire about, place exchanges, and track positions.

Here's our recommendation on finding an intermediary that offers the administration and the features that best serve your options trading needs.

1. Search for free training

In case you're new to options trading or need to grow your trading procedures, finding a firm that has assets for teaching clients is an unquestionable requirement. That training can come in numerous structures, including:

Online options trading courses.

Live or recorded online classes.

One-on-one direction on the web or by telephone

Eye-to-eye gatherings with a bigger firm that has branches nationwide.

It's a smart thought to spend some time in understudy driver mode and absorb as much training and guidance as you can. Stunningly better, if a dealer offers a reenacted variant of its options trading stage, test-drive the procedure with a paper trading account before putting any genuine money on hold.

2. Put your agent's client support to the test

Solid client support ought to be a high need, especially for more current options merchants. It's likewise significant for the individuals who are exchanging brokers or leading complex exchanges with which they may need assistance.

Think about what sort of getting in touch you like. Live online talk? Email? Telephone support? Does the agent have a committed trading work area on call? What hours is it staffed? Is specialized help accessible every minute of every day or just weekdays? Should not something be said about delegates who can address inquiries regarding your record?

Indeed, even before you apply for a record, connect and pose a few inquiries to check whether the appropriate responses and reaction time are good.

3. Ensure the trading stage is anything but difficult to utilize

Options trading platforms come in all shapes and sizes. They can be web or programming based, work area or online just, have separate platforms for essential and propelled trading, offer full or incomplete versatile usefulness, or a mix of the above.

Visit an agent's site and search for a guided voyage through its foundation and apparatuses. Screen captures, and video instructional exercises are pleasant, however, evaluating a merchant's reenacted trading stage, on the off chance that it has one, will give you the best feeling of whether the intermediary is a solid match.

A few interesting points:

Is the stage structure easy to use or do you need to chase and peck to discover what you need?

How simple is it to make an exchange?

Could the stage do the things you need, such as making cautions dependent on explicit criteria or giving you a chance to round out an exchange ticket in advance to submit later?

Will you need portable access to the full suite of administrations when you're in a hurry, or will a pared-down adaptation of the stage do the trick?

How solid is the site, and how rapidly are requests executed? This is a high need if your strategy includes rapidly entering and leaving positions.

Does the specialist charge a month to month or yearly stage expense? Assuming this is the case, are there approaches to get the expense postponed, for example, keeping a base record equalization or directing a specific number of exchanges during a particular period?

4. Survey the expansiveness, profundity, and cost of information and instruments

Information and research are a options merchant's soul. A portion of the nuts and bolts to search for:

An as often as possible updated statements feed.

Fundamental graphing to help pick your entrance and leave positions.

The capacity to examine an exchange's potential risks and rewards (most extreme upside and greatest drawback).

Screening devices.

Those wandering into further developed trading methodologies may require further expository and exchange displaying apparatuses, for example, adjustable screeners; the capacity to assemble, test, track and back-test trading systems; and continuous market information from various suppliers.

Verify whether the extravagant stuff costs extra. For instance, most brokers give free deferred statements, falling 20 minutes behind market information, yet charge an expense for a constant feed. Also, some star level apparatuses might be accessible just to clients who meet month to month or quarterly trading action or record balance essentials.

5. Try not to gauge the cost of commissions too intensely

There's an explanation bonus expenses are lower on our rundown. Cost isn't all that matters, and it's positively not as significant as the different things we've covered. But since commissions give an advantage next to the other correlation, they regularly are the principal things individuals see when picking an options specialist.

A couple of things to think about how much brokers charge to exchange options:

The two segments of an options trading commission are the base rate, basically equivalent to the thing as the trading commission that investors pay when they purchase a stock, and the per-contract expense. Commissions typically go from $3 to $9.99 per exchange, with contract expenses running from 15 pennies to $1.25 or more.

A few brokers pack the trading commission and the per-contract expense into a solitary level charge.

A few brokers additionally offer limited commissions dependent on trading recurrence, volume, or normal record balance — the meaning of "high volume" or "dynamic merchant" shifts by the investor.

In case you're new to options trading or utilize the strategy just sparingly, you'll be well-served by picking either an expedite that offers a solitary level rate to exchange or one that charges a commission in addition to per-contract expense. In case you're an increasingly dynamic merchant, you should survey your trading rhythm to check whether a layered evaluating plan would set aside your cash.

Obviously, the less you pay in charges, the more benefit you keep. However, we should put things in context: Platform expenses, information expenses, inertia charges, and fill-in-the-clear charges can occur without much of a stretch could counterbalance the reserve funds you may get from going with an expedite that charges a couple of bucks less for commissions.

There's another potential issue in the event that you base your option exclusively on commissions. Rebate brokers can charge absolute bottom costs since they give just no frills platforms or attach additional expenses for information and apparatuses. Then again, at a portion of the bigger, increasingly settled brokers you'll pay higher commissions, however, in return you get free access to all the data you have to perform due to perseverance.

Best Options Trading Brokers and Platforms

Options trading has turned out to be amazingly prominent with retail investors in recent years. Our best options brokers have an abundance of instruments, including portfolio margining, that help you measure and oversee risk as you figure out which exchanges to put. They likewise incorporate significant instruction that encourages you to develop in modernity as an options dealer. Here are our top brokers in the business for options trading:

- TD AMERITRADE (THINKORSWIM)

- ROBINHOOD

- E-TRADE

- INTERACTIVE BROKERS

- TRADESTATION

- ALLY INVEST

- CHARLES SCHWAB (STREETSMART PLATFORMS)

- LIGHTSPEED

TD Ameritrade (thinkorswim)

TD Ameritrade takes the top spot in this positioning thanks to a combination of sensible evaluating, brilliant fledgling assets, and a best-in-class trading stage that functions admirably for specialists and expert dealers. Regardless of where you are in your options trading venture, TD Ameritrade has something for everybody.

Exchanges at TD Ameritrade cost $6.95 per exchange in addition to $0.75 per contract. There is no record least. The site offers a present promotion where you get 60 days of without commission value, ETF, and options exchanges with a deposit of $3,000 or more. You gets extra rewards with bigger opening balances.

Novices have a wide scope of assets that are incredible for options and other investing and trading techni☐ues. For master merchants, the Think or Swim stage gives you Wall Street Quality at a Main Street cost.

The thinkorswim stage is most appropriate for further developed options dealers, with an assortment of options option devices and risk management. You can assemble your very own specialized examinations from more than 500 markers in both the downloadable stage and its going with portable application.

TD Ameritrade likewise got honors for Best Overall Online Brokers, Best for Day Trading, Best Web Trading Platforms, Best for Beginners, Best for ETFs, Best for Roth IRAs, Best for IRAs, and Best Stock Trading Apps.

Pros

Top notch training, including live content on TDAmeritradeNetwork.com.

Practice options trading systems utilizing a trading test system.

thinkorswim stage has dynamite apparatuses for choosing options systems.

Gushing information accessible on all platforms.

Cons

Higher than normal commissions and per-contract expense.

Extremely high edge rates.

The intricacy of the thinkorswim stage makes a few highlights hard to discover.

Having options devices spread more than two unique platforms is awkward.

Robinhood

You can't get less expensive than free. While some expert dealers are not content with how exchanges are taken care of and handled at Robinhood, it is a great stage for amateurs to begin with - less risk. With no trading expense, you can purchase and sell options without risking anything over your underlying investment.

Robinhood is a web-first stage, and it doesn't offer much with regards to instruction and research apparatuses. In any case, if you read a book on options and need to attempt your hand as a pro, Robinhood can positively deal with your needs.

Robinhood additionally offers without commission stock exchanges, ETFs, a predetermined number of cryptocurrencies, and a set number of ADRs (American Depository Receipts — a sort of stock posting in the US for an outside organization). Since it is versatile first, it offers incredible continuous warnings for investments and exchanges on the stage.

ETRADE (Power ETRADE)

ETrade is the most established online financier, and it has a long history of supporting both apprentice and master level brokers. Through its committed OptionsHouse stage, you can locate a wide scope of information and research instruments that incorporate devices to manufacture propelled options chains and trading stepping stools.

While it is a rebate financier, commissions are not the most minimal on the rundown. Exchanges cost $6.95 in addition to $0.75 per contract. Be that as it may, a few limits apply for high volume dealers. Value and list options drop to $4.95 per exchange and $0.50 per contract with at least 30 exchanges for each □uarter.

With a new record that gets a deposit of $10,000 or more, you'll get up to $600 in free exchanges and 60 days of no commission exchanges. That is a really decent arrangement to kick you off. With ETrade and others, generally, consider how exchange charges cut into your benefits after some time.

Despite the fact that you approach a abundance of investigation and research on the great E*TRADE stage, you'll need to flip over to discover those highlights.

ETRADE additionally got honors for Best Web Trading Platforms, Best for ETFs, Best Stock Trading Apps, Best for Roth IRAs, Best for IRAs, and Best for Beginners.

Pros

Graphing and estimating devices in the Power E*Trade stage are an option.

Adjustable options chains and trading stepping stools.

Visit merchants meet all requirements for lower base commissions.

Cons

Higher-than-normal commissions and per-contract charge.

High edge rates.

Multi-leg spreads bring about an extra base commission charge.

Interactive Brokers

This broker had a long-standing reputation for low costs, a troublesome stage, and horrible administration that obliged hyperactive merchants. However, that reputation has changed much in the last three to four years as the firm sought after less dynamic and less complex clients. The organization's Trader Workstation stage, accessible as either a downloadable bundle or a site, has turned out to be friendlier and increasingly adaptable. Their portable applications are intended to work with least composing, rather, using haggles directions.

A generally new highlight, IBot, gives you a chance to pose inquiries in plain English and get a brisk answer, instead of burrowing around the stage. For instance, you can ask IBot to show a specific strike and expiry date by composing (or saying) "Show options chain for GOOG for the following three expirations."

Options brokers can set up a spread rapidly and move it to a future expiry with only two or three ticks. IB's Probability Lab gives you a chance to reproduce a potential exchange before utilizing genuine money.

You can just show spilling cites on each gadget in turn, so in the event that you have the site up on your computer, and, at that point sign in to your portable application, one stage will be automatically limited to depiction cites. Records with under $100,000 in assets pay a base expense of $10/month, and may need to pay extra charges for continuous information. The web adaptation of Trader Workstation does not have a portion of the highlights in the downloadable stage; however all watchlists and alarms are shared.

Interactive Brokers additionally got honors for Best Overall Online Brokers, Best for International Stock Trading, Best for Low Costs, Best for Penny Stocks, and Best for Day Trading.

Pros

No record least and no per-leg base expense.

Edge rates are the most minimal of all brokers overviewed.

Many options-arranged exercises.

Cons

Gushing statements show on each gadget in turn.

Client support is improving yet, at the same time has a reputation for being lazy.

TradeStation

TradeStation began as a product organization for merchants, and despite the fact that it has developed after some time, it has maintained its underlying trading standards. In the event that you need proficient information and fast exchange execution on a specialist level stage, TradeStation is an extraordinary decision.

TradeStation charges $5 per exchange in addition to $0.50 per contract. Be that as it may, it additionally offers unbundled and per-contract evaluating. Expert and high-volume dealers may improve the level rate cost of $1 per contract rather than the base + per contract expense most financiers charge.

While it doesn't offer as much for novice merchants and new brokers, you could have a family office or business portfolio on TradeStation without any issues. Truth be told, its instruments are so great it offers a significant number of them for a charge to proficient investors with records at different brokers. With a functioning record at TradeStation, you get those apparatuses for nothing. Simply be careful as the base $2,000 parity or five exchanges for every year to maintain a strategic distance from a $95 yearly record expense.

Ally invest

Ally Invest is another minimal effort business best known for its cousin Ally Bank. Like the bank, Ally Invest offers a straightforward and low-charge business lineup. Exchanges are $4.95 each in addition to $0.65 per contract. There is no record minumum. With a present advancement, you can get up to $3,500 reward money depending on the size of your store.

You can begin with a low investment to become familiar with Ally without stressing over huge least adjusts or charges. Be that as it may, even some increasingly experienced brokers will be content with the low costs and a wide scope of administrations intended for option merchants.

Features incorporate an incredible trading stage and important graphs, information, and examination to enable you to assemble your options trading strategy. In the realm of markdown financiers, you can't generally take the value of a merchant from its trading expenses. At Ally, that is surely the situation.

Lightspeed

Lightspeed is a specialist intended to address the issues of experienced and exceptionally dynamic options brokers. Lightspeed gives a committed options-trading stage (Livevol X) and a few options diagnostic devices, for example, verifiable options Greeks and slants information, not offered by different brokers. A variety of scanners in the Lightspeed Trader stage help spot trading openings, and the stage's progressed diagramming highlights are very adaptable.

For portfolio investigation, you can bunch your situations by basic image, which enables productive merchants to figure out which procedures are working. You'll likewise discover a benefit and loss risk graph for complex methodologies. The stage performed very well during the ongoing trading floods.

Versatile and electronic applications, however, don't permit futures trading or direct market get to. This isn't a fitting stage for new options brokers.

Lightspeed got honors for the best when it comes to low Costs and Best for Day Trading.

Pros

Per-contract commissions rate is very low (with no per-leg base charge).

Staggering request execution programming produces value improvement.

Livevol X stage has no month to month charge.

Cons

High parity required to open a record.

Lightspeed Trader stage has a base $100/month charge.

Restricted instructive contributions.

Charles Schwab (StreetSmart platforms)

Charles Schwab conveys an inside and out incredible involvement with fantastic client support. When you open another record, exchanges are $.95 each in addition to $0.65 per contract. First-time customers get 500 no commission exchanges for a long time when you store $100,000 or more in another record.

Schwab offers better than expected research and training contributions. It additionally gives you a generally excellent stage for trading on work area, web, and versatile. Indeed, even outside of options it is extraordinary compared to other by and large financiers for a wide scope of investing and trading needs.

With the enormous library of instructive and research content, you can enter the fast options trading world with your eyes wide open to the risks and openings. All things considered, the aggressive expenses and quality trading platforms make it a commendable consideration for even the most experienced dealers. Records requires a $1,000 least to get to options trading.

This is a decent stage for the rising options broker, with a lot of help and instruction. The expenses are on the low side too. For progressively refined options dealers, a device demonstrates how a speculative exchange would influence your edge balance.

Charles Schwab likewise got honors for Best Overall Online Brokers, Best Web Trading Platforms, Best for International Trading, Best for Penny Stocks, Best for Beginners, Best for Roth IRAs, Best for IRAs, Best for ETFs, and Best Stock Trading Apps.

Pros

The Idea Hub in the StreetSmart platforms shows noteworthy trading thoughts.

Options-situated trading exercises that develop with you.

A wide exhibit of asset classes can be exchanged on any of the accessible platforms.

Cons

The multiplication of platforms disperses options determination devices in better places.

Altering portfolio examination pages to show options-explicit execution is awkward.

Edge rates are higher than normal.

Tastyworks

A stage worked for regular options merchants, tastyworks is the business ally to tastytrade, a cheeky budgetary news and instruction stage. There are three different ways to get to the stage: a groundbreaking downloadable bundle, a site, and versatile applications. The firm charges commissions just for opening a position, urging their clients to escape level exchanges.

There are a couple of more fancy odds and ends in the downloadable rendition; however, the others aren't missing much. The majority of the apparatuses are intended to get you concentrated on liquidity, likelihood, and volatility. This financier opened in January 2017, so it's not burdened with heritage frameworks that hinder huge numbers of the more seasoned businesses. Executions are quick, and the expenses are low, especially with the evaluating change declared in July 2018 that tops value option exchange commissions at $10 per leg. Despite the fact that a newcomer to options trading may be initially awkward, the individuals who comprehend the fundamental ideas will value the substance and highlights. Tastyworks likewise got honors for Best for Day Trading and Best for Low Costs.

Pros

Entirely steady stage.

Every one of the apparatuses are open from a solitary page.

The stage is centered around derivatives trading.

Cons

Newcomers might be overpowered.

Some asset classes are inaccessible.

Restricted portfolio examination.

Opening a options trading account

Before you can even begin, you need to clear a couple of obstacles. Due to the measure of capital re uired and the multifaceted nature of foreseeing numerous moving parts, brokers need to discover more about a potential investor before granting them a consent slip to begin trading options.

Brokerage firms screen potential options dealers to evaluate their trading knowledge, their comprehension of the risks in options, and their budgetary readiness.

Opening a brokerage record doesn't mean you can begin trading options. Despite everything, you need endorsement before you can even begin thinking of a strategy. Brokerage firms rate their customers on a scale.

The regular scale runs 1 to 5. Yet, a few spots, similar to Charles Schwab, take a shot at their own scale. As a rule, the scales go from low to high in this technique:

Covered calls

Purchase calls and puts

Spreads

Uncovered calls/puts

Each level is aggregate. On the off chance that you are appraised at Level 2, you can likewise exchange whatever Level 1 can exchange. The higher you proceed onward the scale, the more you can exchange.

Your affirmed level relies upon an assortment of components:

Money related destinations: Are you attempting to develop your income or keep up your capital?

Investment goals, for example, income, development, capital conservation, or speculation

Involvement in the market: Are you a prepared dealer? What sorts of protections have you purchased/sold? Have you at any point purchased/sold options previously? What number of exchanges do you make every year?

Trading background, including your insight into investing, to what extent you've been trading stocks or options, what number of exchanges you make every year and the size of your exchanges

Risk resistance: Do you have strong work? It is safe to say that you are risking the majority of your capital or only a small amount of it? Brokers may even get some information about your yearly income and absolute total assets. They need a strong thought of the risks you are happy to take. Individual budgetary data, including total fluid assets (or investments effectively sold for money), yearly income, all out total assets, and work data

This data enables brokers to choose which option trading level suits you. Each trading level permits a particular kind of options exchanges. Be that as it may, the permitted exchanges at each level could change by agent. Approach your agent for a rundown of each level so you can see where you stand.

Sorts OF OPTIONS

Most of options exchanged on the market are list or individual security options. The options anticipate either how a noteworthy file, similar to the S&P 500, will do, or how a particular basic stock will perform. These are the fundamental exchanges.

However, it's additionally conceivable to exchange ETF and forex options. ETFs track a particular market fragment, for instance, precious stones. On the off chance that you have an enthusiasm for the precious stones market, you could exchange ETF options this market fragment. You can likewise expand your risks and purchase options on the forex market.

PUT YOUR PREDICTORS' CAP ON

When you comprehend the essentials of options trading, it's a great opportunity to decide. It begins with foreseeing a stock's heading.

There are three center components you ought to consider.

What do you figure the stock will do?

You should decide whether you think the stock will go up or down. This will help decide the correct strategy for options trading.

If you foresee the stock cost will build, you'll purchase a call. This gives you the right, not the commitment, to purchase the stock at the strike cost. When the stock's market cost surpasses your strike value, you are in-the-money. You'll purchase the stock at the lower strike cost and sell it at the higher market cost. You benefit is the difference less any commissions paid.

If you anticipate the stock cost will diminish, you'll purchase a put. This gives you the right, not the commitment, to sell the stock at the strike cost. When the stock's market cost is beneath your strike value, you are in-the-money. You could purchase the stock at the lower market cost and afterward sell it at the higher strike cost. The difference less commission paid is your benefit.

If the stock's market cost doesn't move like you figured, the option could lapse "out-of-the-money." If you purchased a call and the stock's market cost did not surpass the strike cost at expiration, it's out-of-the-money. If you purchased a put, and the stock's market cost surpasses the strike value, it's out-of-the-money. These are the real risks associated with buying options.

What amount do you figure the stock cost will change?

This will enable you to decide the correct strike cost.

Picking the correct strike cost isn't as overpowering as it appears. The strike costs are institutionalized. You'll see an assortment of accessible strike costs; however, they will consistently be in explicit augmentations. The common additions incorporate $1, $5, and $10. Occasionally, you may likewise observe $2.50 increases. The institutionalized additions remove a little mystery from the procedure.

A call is "in-the-money" when the market cost is higher than the call's strike cost.

A put is "in-the-money" when the market cost is lower than the put's strike cost.

What extent do you think the stock's cost will move?

This is the place taking a gander at the stock's chronicled examples satisfies. Realizing the stock's history can give you a thought of when you figure the stock's cost will change.

You can just browse the accessible expiration dates. You can generically decide how long you think a stock will take to change.

If you think a stock will change in the short-term, you could consider a month to month expiration, regardless of whether 1, 3, or a half year.

If you think a stock will take more time to transform, you could consider a yearly expiration.

Specialized ANALYSIS

Anticipating an option's future re□uires a touch of specialized examination. You'll need to comprehend the following:

Bolster levels: This is the stock's normal "depressed spot." Relying on on the stock to go underneath this point could be risky.

Opposition levels: This is the stock's regular "high point." Relying on the stock to go over this point could be risky.

Volume: As you track the stock's history, you'll need to take a gander at the volume behind it. The more offers exchanged at a specific value, the more probable it's a pattern. Depending on low volumes could lead you off course.

You can become familiar with these levels by perusing the stock's graph designs. Take a gander at its history, concentrating on explicit examples. Your brokerage firm should enable you to get familiar with these components, and that's just the beginning.

Concentrating on these variables will enable you to decide whether you should purchase/sell a put or call; the strike cost; and the expiration date.

For instance, if you think stock costs are going to build, you need to purchase a call. This gives you the privilege to purchase the stock of the basic protections at the strike cost. This ought to be beneath the market value. You would then make a benefit.

Then again, if you figure stock costs may fall, you'd purchase a put. This gives you a agreement to sell the stock at a more expensive rate than the market value.

Foreseeing the expansion/decline re□uires research and learning, however. This is the place the correct merchant proves to be useful. They'll give you the exploration you have to choose. What did the stock do historically? What are the general sentiments towards the stock today? You'll likewise need to comprehend the stock's implied volatility. Your agent can enable you to comprehend the risks in □uestion.

Finally, you'll have to pick an expiration date. The farther the expiration date, the more prominent the time value of the option. As such, the longer the stock needs to increase or reduce, contingent upon what you're seeking after to make a benefit. Keep in mind, the longer the expiration, the more prominent the premium.

Setting your first trading on options

Setting your first options exchange isn't as hard as it might appear. You'll never learn until you do it so how about we stroll through putting your first exchange step-by-step.

Toward the part of the arrangement instructional exercise, include your remarks and let me know whether you think this was useful in kicking you off or not.

Firstly: Login To Your Brokerage Account

I accept that you as of now have an extraordinary specialist and can either login on the web or download a work area application. In any case, to put a trade, you have to gain admittance to the market.

I'll be utilizing TD Ameritrade (thinkorswim) for this down to earth example.

Next: Discover The "order" or "trade" Page

A few brokers will have tabs or pages where every one of the orders are finished. Discover this page - it's most likely unmistakably named because they need you trading.

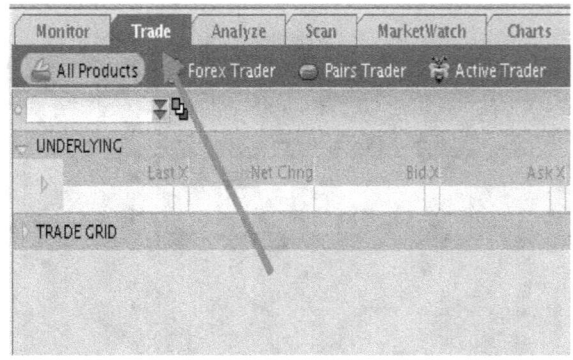

Next: Draw Up A Stock/ETF Quote

Type in a ticker image to draw up the live market cites for the stock/ETF you might want to trade options on. In this model, I'll simply utilize AAPL for Apple Stock.

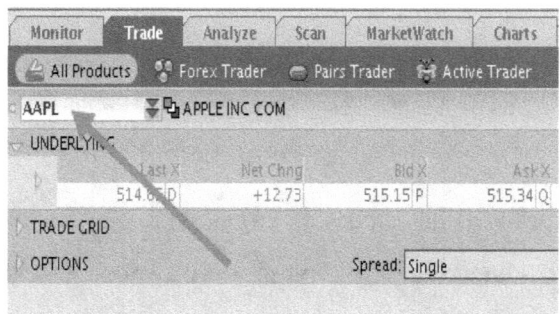

Next: Quest For The Options Quote Table

When the statements start spilling in, there will be both the "basic" and "options" cites. Pick the options.

Next: Pick Your Expiration Month

Presently you need to choose with the month you need to trade - the front month or close to month. Front month options are the following month terminate. For our situation, these will be March.

		CALLS					Strikes:
Mark	Volu	Ope	Prob	ROC	Bid X	Ask X	Exp
FEB4 12 (3) 100 (Weeklys)							
MAR 12 (24) 100							
21.40	8,649	9,697	58.74%	N/A	21.30 A	21.50 X	MAR 12
18.50	16,537	13,771	53.76%	N/A	18.45 X	18.55 Q	MAR 12
15.85	14,957	7,629	48.72%	N/A	15.80 X	15.90 X	MAR 12
13.55	12,075	11,895	43.72%	N/A	13.50 A	13.60 Q	MAR 12
11.35	7,449	7,426	38.79%	N/A	11.30 X	11.40 W	MAR 12
9.55	7,688	8,587	34.12%	N/A	9.50 N	9.60 Q	MAR 12
APR 12 (59) 100							
30.125	1,433	6,293	54.28%	N/A	29.95 A	30.30 X	APR 12
27.375	3,035	7,197	51.07%	N/A	27.25 Q	27.50 A	APR 12
24.80	1,673	4,126	47.85%	N/A	24.65 X	24.95 A	APR 12
22.425	1,463	6,104	44.65%	N/A	22.30 Q	22.55 A	APR 12
20.175	1,826	8,350	41.49%	N/A	20.05 A	20.30 A	APR 12
18.075	1,926	4,308	38.39%	N/A	17.95 X	18.20 X	APR 12
MAY 12 (87) 100							
36.10	416	1,276	52.44%	N/A	35.90 B	36.30 X	MAY 12
33.50	674	1,988	49.84%	N/A	33.35 Z	33.65 A	MAY 12
30.90	418	1,381	47.27%	N/A	30.75 N	31.05 X	MAY 12
28.40	588	1,934	44.70%	N/A	28.30 I	28.50 N	MAY 12
26.15	311	1,261	42.16%	N/A	26.00 X	26.30 X	MAY 12
23.975	288	1,531	39.66%	N/A	23.85 I	24.10 A	MAY 12

Next: Select Your Strike Price

Down the center of the valuing table will be all the distinctive strike costs for the two Calls and Puts. Look down and pick the strike value that you need.

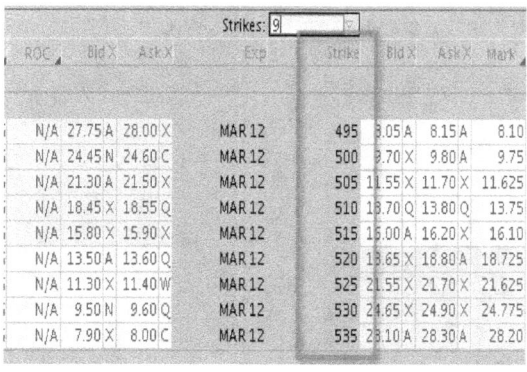

Next: Pick Either "Call" or "Put."

Typically the Calls will be recorded on the left and the Puts on the privilege on the right. Locate the side of the trade you need to be on and hit the offered/request that statements draw up the genuine order structure for the option. Keep in mind that BID = Sell and ASK = Buy

Next: Enter The Quantity

Basic enough right, simply enter the quantity of contracts you need to trade.

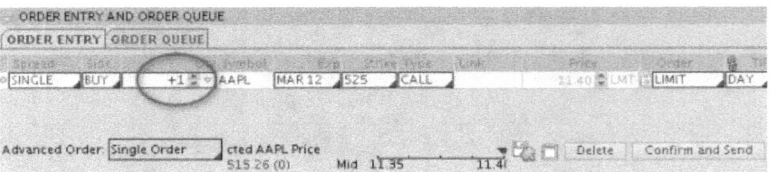

Next: Set You Desired Price

Again, set the cost to what you need to pay for the option.

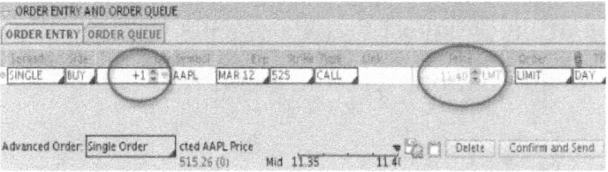

Next: Pick The Order Type

The order type is a further developed element that I've covered in other video instructional exercises. For our motivations, we are going to utilize a LIMIT order that pegs the value we are happy to pay- the value we enter.

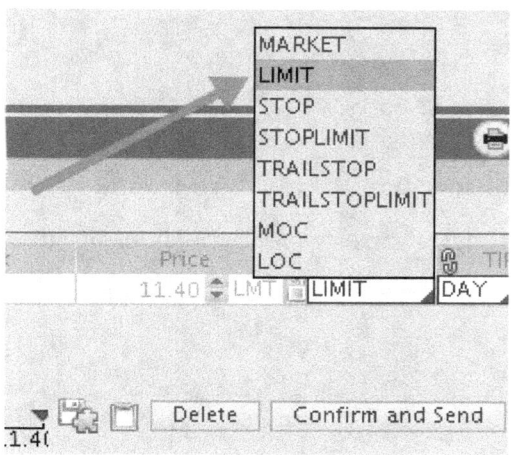

Next: DAY or GTC?

This will decide to what extent the order will remain open if it's not filled. Day orders unmistakably remain open only the day and automatically drop at the market close. GTC orders are "Great Til Cancelled" which means they will remain open and working until they are filled, or you drop it yourself.

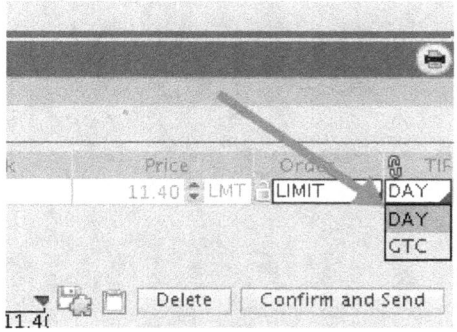

Next: Confirm and Send!

Take 1 moment and go over your order again ensuring that everything is right. Ensure you are entering the correct cost and amount. Only a brief period checking your orders will spare you a large number of dollars every year.

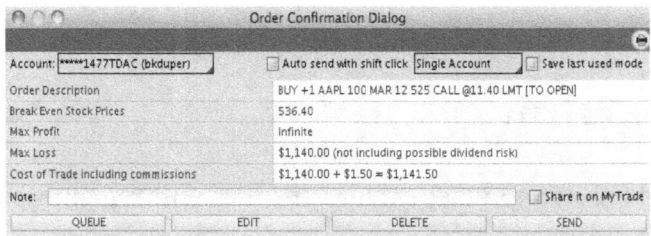

That is it; You just place your first options trade, wasn't that simpler than you thought?

CONCLUSION

Options trading might seem frustrating, but they're clear to see once you learn a few tips. Investor portfolios are often constructed with different asset sessions. These could be stocks and shares, bonds, ETFs, and also mutual funds. Options are another property class, so, when used correctly, they provide several benefits that stock trading and ETFs only cannot.

www.ingramcontent.com/pod-product-compliance
Lightning Source LLC
Chambersburg PA
CBHW070631220526
45466CB00001B/148